Heavenly
visions

Dedication

Dedicated to my precious brother Micah Drew White who stepped before me into eternity along with other ancestry such as Rolene Jordan, Willa Aleta White, Viola Badgett, and JoAnn Johns. This glimpse of Heaven is from all the loved ones who went before to all of those remaining!

Written by: Donesa Walker
Design by: Will Baten
Edited by: Kelley Inderman

Contents

While he was trying to figure a way out, he had a dream. God's angel spoke in the dream: "Joseph, son of David, don't hesitate to get married. Mary's pregnancy is Spirit-conceived. God's Holy Spirit has made her pregnant. She will bring a son to birth, and when she does, you, Joseph, will name him Jesus—'God saves'—because he will save his people from their sins." This would bring the prophet's embryonic revelation to full term:
Watch for this—a virgin will get
pregnant and bear a son;
They will name him Immanuel
(Hebrew for "God is with us").
Then Joseph woke up. He did exactly what God's angel commanded in the dream: He married Mary. But he did not consummate the marriage until she had the baby. He named the baby Jesus.

Matthew 1: 20-25

Woke!

While he was trying to figure a way out, Joseph had a dream; then he woke up and did exactly what God commanded in the dream. These are powerful words. We miss this so often as we read through scriptures and stroll through life. God reveals Himself to us and we let the revelation go as we move onto other things in our day to day. We release the vision/dream without action. I am positive that there were many people who spoke a lot of negativity into the lives of Mary/Joseph throughout their raising of Jesus but they both had an experience with God and held onto that experience for the duration.

The gospels of the new covenant of Jesus with His bride open with a lineage of Joseph although biologically speaking, he was not the father of Jesus. Lineage is an important piece of ancestry and documents the bloodline. Although Mary was also of the house of David, when lineage is recorded in Matthew, it is that of Joseph that God records in scripture. It is believed by most Biblical scholars that Mary's lineage is that which is recorded in Luke's gospel. While lineage is important to establish the throne of David or royalty and the house of Judah flowed through both lines of parentage, the most significant aspect of the gospels isn't the parentage but the presence of the Spirit.

We can be raised in the ways of God and know who God is but it is our own experience with God that creates the choice of action. Joseph and Mary both were raised in the knowledge of God, in Biblical Jewish law and tradition. We see through scripture the character of both of these individuals but we often overlook what actions they took with their dreams/visions. In today's culture, being Woke means socially aware of cultural diversity. It has a negative connotation to some and positive to others because it depicts a person who is aware of cultural identity and societal norms that are in defiance of God's laws. Let's be honest. When Joseph woke up from his dream, he had to confront reality just as we do daily. He had a choice to make which we each do. That choice is, what do we do about Jesus? Jesus was already a person of Earthly birth, alive as a king immortal inhabited in the womb of Mary as an unborn babe at the time of Joseph's dream. Joseph and Mary were legally married and it was time for him to receive his bride into his home according to their culture when Joseph was told of Mary's condition. Joseph, being a good man, was trying to decide how to quickly and quietly extricate himself from an unhappy circumstance when he had his dream from God. He was troubled, weighted, stressed, overwhelmed, overburdened and disappointed. He had experienced a letdown and a circumstance of a huge problem. He was caught in a no win situation but had no idea that God had designed and planned that circumstance for just that time. All he saw was the problems and while trying to resolve a solution, he had a dream. The dream is rightly a God given dream but the importance is the next step of action. When Joseph woke, he chose action. He chose to do exactly as God's angel commanded in the dream. How powerful this is! We don't hear a lot about Joseph in the Bible. He is a character of background and steadiness in scripture. Some project that he passed away prior to Jesus' earthly ministry although we do know he trained Jesus in cultural ways and as a carpenter from the records. My concern isn't with what happened next in Joseph's life but in what he did about Jesus. This is the same question we all have to answer. What will you do about Jesus? We all have dreams/visions. We all have problems and dilemmas. We all have situations that dissatisfy, confuse, frustrate and leave us feeling lost and betrayed. We all have a choice when we wake up each day. What will we do about Jesus? Joseph did exactly what God commanded in the dream. His family, friends and advisers were probably confused and wondering what he was thinking but he made a choice to follow what God had shown him. His choice was what he did about Jesus. Joseph holds a place in history that is highly valued because when he woke up, he chose to do as God commanded in the dream. Cultural wars rage. Wokeness is a very real term that threatens our very existence. We have a choice to make daily as we wake from our slumber. What will we do about Jesus? Will He take an important role in our life as we follow what God commands or will we succumb to cultural wars and ways? Will we allow the world to dominate our thoughts and interests, our actions and our ways or will we do as God commands when times become challenging? What will we do about Jesus?
It is time to wake up from our slumber. The choice is ours. What will we do about Jesus today?

Instructed by the king, they set off. Then the star appeared again, the same star they had seen in the eastern skies. It led them on until it hovered over the place of the child. They could hardly contain themselves: They were in the right place! They had arrived at the right time!

Matthew 2:9-10

Right!

Matthew 2 is the story of the wisemen visiting Jesus and the fulfillment of multiple prophecies made hundreds of years before Jesus was born by prophets of old. What struck me as I read this again was the timing significance. The Star the 3 scholars had followed has disappeared. God had shut the light off for a reason. And now after the visit to the king to ask about the fulfillment of prophecy, the star appears again, right on time (almost as if God knew exactly the right time/place!). Then it led them to the exact place where Jesus lived with Mary and Joseph. I do not know exactly the place nor the age of Jesus. People debate whether he was a toddler at this point-we do know he was somewhere under two years because Herod uses that timeline to kill all the boy babies under two in Bethlehem and surrounding areas to fulfill another prophetic word about Rachel lamenting for her children. Multiple prophetic words are fulfilled in this one chapter but grab this word with me: right! When the men arrived with their gifts, they could hardly contain themselves because they were in the right place at the right time! I honestly love that feeling of the right place/right time. It is such a fulfilling feeling! I have had this experience many times in my life when I met the Lord at the right place at the right time and every-time the joy is unspeakable and undeniable. This is why they could hardly contain themselves. It was an orchestral master-piece of a moment with the king of kings. It was a fulfilling experience of a lifelong dream and an arduous journey to see this babe and know that He was the Messiah who would one day rule the nations. Rightness. It is a feeling of completeness and fulfillment. Right place and right time! These scholars trusted a star to guide them but we have the Spirit of God who dwells in us giving us continuous feedback and satisfaction of completeness in Him. We are the stars guiding others to the place where Jesus is. We are His, used by Him, directed by Him and turned into a shining light by Him. You may feel like your light is off and all is dark around you but His word dwells in you. His promises are always true. You see the rain-bow is God's promise and it is always there but we can only see it during/after a storm be-cause the light refraction through water is how we see the beauty. Just because you cannot see the star shining or the rainbow sparkling in the sky doesn't mean it doesn't exist. When times are darkest, hold on. The storms will clear and the promise will be revealed. The night may be long, but at the right time and in the right place, God will light the star again. Dig deep into His word and follow the instructions there. Listen to His voice as He speaks to you. He is here in our midst turning lives around and guiding us to the right place/time of fulfillment of prophecy.

When John realized that a lot of Pharisees and Sadducees were showing up for a baptismal experience because it was becoming the popular thing to do, he exploded: "Brood of snakes! What do you think you're doing slithering down here to the river? Do you think a little water on your snakeskins is going to make any difference? It's your life that must change, not your skin! And don't think you can pull rank by claiming Abraham as father. Being a descendant of Abraham is neither here nor there. Descendants of Abraham are a dime a dozen. What counts is your life. Is it green and flourishing? Because if it's deadwood, it goes on the fire.

"I'm baptizing you here in the river, turning your old life in for a kingdom life. The real action comes next: The main character in this drama—compared to him I'm a mere stagehand—will ignite the kingdom life within you, a fire within you, the Holy Spirit within you, changing you from the inside out. He's going to clean house—make a clean sweep of your lives. He'll place everything true in its proper place before God; everything false he'll put out with the trash to be burned."

Matthew 3: 7-12

Fad!

It is that time of year...the snakes have come out of hibernation and almost everywhere there is water, you can see snakeskin lying at the edge as they surfaced to shed then slithered off. John the Baptist compared religious Christianity to this. At the time, John's gospel message had turned into a popular thing-a fad, a trend, or what we would've seen a lot of-a FB moment, or TikTok dare. John was baptizing people into a new life after repentance and he was paving the way for Jesus' message of the Holy Spirit indwelling. Just before Jesus came to be baptized, the religious leaders of the day decided to dip their toes in the water but John compared them to snakes shedding skins but not changing. In nature, mottling, shedding and transforming happen because God teaches us through His world the principles He laid down in His word. John told these people the truth that ancestry nor bloodline matter. The only thing that matters is growth in Christ. He says, "what counts is your life. Is it green and flourishing?" Just green isn't enough because there are those who are evergreens. They were raised in the ways of God and know them. They attend church, pray and pay tithes but they do not flourish. They simply maintain, always preaching to others about how bad the world is and that they need to change but they themselves have become a stagnant pool with sour water, because they spend less time growing in the word and applying His love and joy as their garments than they do criticizing others about their choices and lifestyles. The real action is the fire. The real action is the Holy Spirit. How are you known? Jesus said that His people will be known by His love. Here he sets a measurement down for us. This measurement is whether we are growing and changing to be more like him or just bushing out ourselves to be more of the same. Do people see Jesus in you? Are you known by His love? Do you spend more time with Him than you do with the news/social media or YouTube/FB? Do people recognize you as His? The fire within burns up the dross, the extra waste of our lives that we continue to indulge in daily, if and only if we surrender fully to Him so that everything false gets put out with the trash when He cleans house. Spring cleanup time is here. Perhaps it is time to reclaim those areas of our hearts and lives that have become cluttered with self. Maybe today is the day to walk down to the River of Life for a fresh dip in His anointing instead of our own ways. Certainly today is a day to worship and praise, sing and shout with joy for He has won the victory over death, hell and the grave. Time for silence and lip service is gone. It is time for the fire of the Holy Spirit to rage within us cleaning the clutter and setting us ablaze in His light, goodness and His love and mercy. His grace is the way. His mercy is new daily. Great is His faithfulness. Time to turn our old lives of fads and fades into kingdom lives full of real action and growth that is flourishing! Fad or fade? Here's a hard question: would you go into this river full of alligators that is in the picture to be baptized with Him? This is the call of new anointing. Are we willing to sacrifice our own lives and lifestyles for more of Him? Fad, fade or Fire?

Jesus answered by quoting Deuteronomy: "It takes more than bread to stay alive. It takes a steady stream of words from God's mouth."

Jesus countered with another citation from Deuteronomy: "Don't you dare test the Lord your God."

Jesus' refusal was curt: "Beat it, Satan!" He backed his rebuke with a third quotation from Deuteronomy: "Worship the Lord your God, and only him. Serve him with absolute single-heartedness."

Matthew 4: 4, 7, 10

Test!

Learning to study is a skill that must be trained. It is the way to be ready when the tests come our way in life. Jesus gave us this example at the beginning of His ministry. Shortly after being baptized by John and before He called His disciples, He was drawn into the wilderness. He knew the test was coming and he studied the Word by praying and fasting for 40 days. Scripture tells us that Satan who was delivering the test also knew that Jesus had fasted so he started the test with a food temptation.

Note: 2 Timothy 2:15 says, "Study to show thyself approved unto God, a workman that needeth not to be ashamed, dividing the word of truth aright." Jesus was showing us the Way to speak The Truth filled with The Light. He demonstrated how to prepare for the test and how to ace it. See that at each of the three tests, Jesus firmly stated the word which answered and deflected the question back. I have heard people say that they don't need the Old Testament because they don't live under the law but the One who came to fulfill all that the law demanded, demonstrated for us that the testament withstands the test. Jesus aced the tests of the physical flesh (the hunger/bread), the second test was a test of the fleshly desire to test and accuse God (jump and let the angels catch you) and the third was the test of human desire for fame and power/authority (you already own it all-just bow). The three truths of these tests all contain one concept that is important: God's word withstands all tests when we serve Him with absoluteness. This is the history lesson that Jesus taught and passed using the word as His weapon of authority. All authority has been given to us to rule over principalities of this Earth but if we allow the fleshly desire for power to take our hearts then we step out from under His authority as heirs to His kingdom. His kingdom isn't about power and might, His kingdom is about love and mercy. His kingdom has power and might but those attributes come from serving under His authority of His love and mercy. Worship with a steady stream of His word and the absolute authority of His might will conquer all tests! Don't rely on the physical and don't allow the things you feel emotionally to drive you. Jesus was hungry after fasting 40 days. I am sure the demands of the physical were extreme and his emotions were all over because he was experiencing all the symptoms we have. He conquered the Esau desire to give up all He had in the spiritual for a moment of physical fulfillment. He conquered the power and authority trap that sidelines so many by remaining in the place of servanthood even to death on the cross. He conquered the final test when He rose again from fighting death, hell and the grave. He conquered all of it through the power of the Word of God and He has given us this same ability but we must study to show ourselves approved as worthy of His hire. From a test comes a testimony.

Beat it Satan! We have got this in the name of Jesus!

"Don't suppose for a minute that I have come to demolish the Scriptures—either God's Law or the Prophets. I'm not here to demolish but to complete. I am going to put it all together, pull it all together in a vast panorama. God's Law is more real and lasting than the stars in the sky and the ground at your feet. Long after stars burn out and earth wears out, God's Law will be alive and working.

"Trivialize even the smallest item in God's Law and you will only have trivialized your-self. But take it seriously, show the way for others, and you will find honor in the kingdom. Unless you do far better than the Pharisees in the matters of right living, you won't know the first thing about entering the kingdom.

Matthew 5: 17-20

Panoramic!

What a moment! What a beautiful view captured by my friend in this panoramic photo. It is almost unreal and unbelievable but he was able to capture the stars of the Milky Way and the wildflowers of the field. I can only imagine when God looks at us with His eye for detail, how it all looks. In Matthew, Jesus speaks saying that He is the one who ties it all together. The Old Testament law and the New Covenant all are satisfied and complete in Him. God's law doesn't fade away but Jesus met the burden of the sacrificial law with His giving of His life. We celebrate the resurrection because it reminds us that He is no longer in the grave and we are alive in Him. He didn't come to demolish the law but rather to complete it once and for all. His word and His laws are like a panoramic view pulling the stars and the flowers of the field into one focus like this photo. God's word is not a trivial thing. It is the completeness of a complex intricacy of interaction. It is the flowers of the fields that breathe the carbon dioxide that we expel and the stars that glisten producing the nitrogen our atmosphere requires. It is that our God knows the most intimate details of our lives and loves us/appreciates us more than anything else. He is closer than the air we breathe. I will confess that lately it seems no one knows me. I have felt very adrift and alone a lot lately because though I am surrounded by others, the intimacy can get lost in the busyness of life. I have had so much to balance that I started focusing on the items I am juggling instead of the One who knows me better than I know myself. We all have these moments of self awareness that shake our understanding of the world and realign us. Sometimes things don't turn out how we hoped or planned. Sometimes our world comes crashing down and we feel lost and hopeless. We begin to focus on the field instead of the Creator. We get stuck on the details rather than the Provider. We get overwhelmed by the mass of expectations instead of realizing that He is the Peace, the Source and our Joy. Life isn't about just making it through and losing all joy while you go through. Life isn't measured by the breath we breathe but rather about moments that take your breath away. Life is about moments....step back. Take a panoramic view of life rather than the moment you are in now. Maybe you want to hold onto this moment because it is special. Or perhaps you want it to pass quickly-because it is stressful. Either way, this moment is a moment God gave you, so you should celebrate it as His moment. When you are feeling overwhelmed, try not to take it out on others but give it to Jesus instead. I often fail at this but I keep trying. Just give it to Him. Yes, people hurt and disappoint you. Yes, you will feel tired, angry, upset, hurt, discouraged, disappointed and stressed. Yes, these emotions are real and they can rock your world but they are like a rock you stub your toe on in this beautiful field of glory. Step back. Breathe. Refocus and see who He is. People fail but Jesus never fails. Worlds fail, economies fail, lives fall apart but He is our Peace. Don't trivialize yourself by missing what you are meant to be. Created in His image for this time, this place and His purpose. Let the disappointment become grains of sand in His hands. He can make them into beautiful glass or into stardust. He can take your moments and make them new if you give them to Him-the good and bad ones.

"Here's what I want you to do: Find a quiet, secluded place so you won't be tempted to role-play before God. Just be there as simply and honestly as you can manage. The focus will shift from you to God, and you will begin to sense his grace.

"The world is full of so-called prayer warriors who are prayer-ignorant. They're full of formulas and programs and advice, peddling techniques for getting what you want from God. Don't fall for that nonsense. This is your Father you are dealing with, and he knows better than you what you need. With a God like this loving you, you can pray very simply. Like this:
Our Father in heaven,
Reveal who you are.
Set the world right;
Do what's best—
as above, so below.
Keep us alive with three square meals.
Keep us forgiven with you and forgiving others.
Keep us safe from ourselves and the Devil.
You're in charge!
You can do anything you want!
You're ablaze in beauty!
Yes. Yes. Yes.

Matthew 6: 6-13

Secluded!

I love waterfalls. They are a symbol of life and a soothing thing to see and hear. If I could have one secluded place to be at peace, it is at the edge, on the bank watching a waterfall. It is peaceful to me because I am outside the chaos that causes the tumbling and churning. When life tumbles and churns, our minds and bodies get all teamed up in emotion and we become overwhelmed so easily. Math has never been my love but I finally understand it because I have learned the principles of formulas and tips/tricks that make it easy. Just like a waterfall, math follows a pattern and Jesus patterned prayer in a simple way in Matthew 6 with The Lord's Prayer. He was telling us that approaching God through Jesus is as simple as acknowledging who He is-Our Father in Heaven, respecting who He is-Hallowed be Your Name, recognizing Why He is-Your kingdom come so Your will shall be done, and relating to Where He is-In Earth as it is in Heaven. He gives us the formula or pattern of asking for forgiveness but also giving forgiveness to others (forgive us our debt as we forgive our debtors) asking for provisions but also sharing our provisions with others (give us this day our daily bread) and asking for help in time of need while recognizing His purpose of testing for the testimony (lead us not into temptation and deliver us from evil). Finally He goes back to reconciliation and reverence-thine is the kingdom, power and glory forever). Many of us grasp this pattern of prayer but miss a really important part. God isn't meeting with us for a formula or a game. He just wants to meet us where we are in simple honesty. He wants us to stay in Him long enough that our focus shifts from the intricately woven details of our lives to the amazing personal God that He is. He wants us to get to the place where we know who He is not who others say He is. Don't fall for patterns or speeches or formulas to meet God. He is our Father. He knows us so much more than we know ourselves and there is no magic in the words or arrangement of words. It is all about this loving God meeting with us in an intimate way. The quiet and seclusion are not about Him as He can hear you in your worst place of chaos. The quiet place is about our need to focus on who He is and not on our circumstances. The waterfalls of life are twisting, churning and crazy as we float them. Often, we feel the turbulence and feel we are going under but if we will step back onto the bank by reaching out to the Peace Speaker, who is the Water-Walker, who is the Storm-Calmer, the One and Only, then we will see the waterfall of life as a place of calm and peace. Joy isn't found in turbulent times but can be had in turbulence. You see in the waterfall of life, there are rocks. These rocks determine the way the water moves because they are unyielding and fixed. They will experience change in the waters of life due to erosion but they remain in the joy of Jesus because they know in Whom they have believed. We know He is able and we know He is willing and we know that He knows what we need before we think or ask, but oh how He loves to hear our voice. Take time to become secluded in His peace and anchored in His presence.

"Here is a simple, rule-of-thumb guide for behavior: Ask yourself what you want people to do for you, then grab the initiative and do it for them. Add up God's Law and Prophets and this is what you get.

"These words I speak to you are not incidental additions to your life, homeowner improvements to your standard of living. They are foundational words, words to build a life on. If you work these words into your life, you are like a smart carpenter who built his house on solid rock. Rain poured down, the river flooded, a tornado hit—but nothing moved that house. It was fixed to the rock.

"But if you just use my words in Bible studies and don't work them into your life, you are like a stupid carpenter who built his house on the sandy beach. When a storm rolled in and the waves came up, it collapsed like a house of cards."

Matthew 7: 12, 24-27

Initiative!

The photo behind this scripture is a little hard to see but it is a photo of a Fountain of Knowledge: a waterfall built around books. The one book that truly is the Fountain of Knowledge is really the Foundation. If you start building with a solid foundation, then you are much more likely to end up with a strong building but what is under the foundation matters. If you are building your foundation on sand that shifts and settles rather than bedrock, your foundation will crack and your house will fail. There is this parable in Matthew of the two men who built their houses: one on a sandy beach that easily collapsed at the first storm and another who secured his foundation to a rock that withstood flooding and tornadoes. Roots matter, strong foundations matter but the principles of God's law is the steady rock. Jesus compares the man who built His house on the rock to a man who uses God's word as a place to build, a rock, a foundation and a solid place to construct life, while just an occasional look, glance or devotional is like a foundation built on shifting sands. If I am building on God's word, how can I know that I am building on the rock and not the sand? The tests of life and time will rock all of us as we will all experience earthquakes and tornadoes, floods and other disasters to our "home" but if we are anchored on the rock, these tests and trials will lead to testimonies not breakdowns. These tests and trials will be moments of development and not moments that undermine. These moments of trial and heartbreak come to all of us but when we know without a doubt that He is greater, then we can walk in confidence of who He is rather than who we are. Ask yourself what it is you want from others and then do it for them. This is the sum total of God's law. His love should be the condition that ignites the initiative within us to be more and do more. It isn't about us. It is about Him. I have been around more than half a century and seen a few things. I have experienced the highs and lows of life in every sense but throughout all, He has been faithful. Have I gotten everything I wanted and desired? Not yet. Have I seen bad things happen to good people and good things go to bad people? Absolutely. Life isn't fair. In this world we will all have trouble but our joy is that we know we are not of this world. We have a rock solid anchor in who He is. We can be satisfied and content with what God provides knowing that through Him and His provisions, we will be made more than conquering kings. Take initiative to be His hand extended. If you are hungry, feed another. If you are thirsty, direct another to the source of Living Water. If you are tired and weary, come to Jesus, rest, refill then take your abilities and go share His mercy and grace with those who are hurting. His initiative is yours-reach out to the hurting and direct them to the King of Peace. If you are grieving and heavy laden, take it to Jesus then let Him turn the dark moments into memories of joy. Do not build on the sand of shifting religious perspectives but rather on the rock of God's principles.

Taken aback, Jesus said, "I've yet to come across this kind of simple trust in Israel, the very people who are supposed to know all about God and how he works. This man is the vanguard of many outsiders who will soon be coming from all directions—streaming in from the east, pouring in from the west, sitting down at God's kingdom banquet alongside Abraham, Isaac, and Jacob. Then those who grew up 'in the faith' but had no faith will find themselves out in the cold, outsiders to grace and wondering what happened."

Matthew 8: 10-12

Vanguard!

Cutting edge, forefront, prominent leader...these are synonyms that still lack in meaning, to the compliment Jesus gave the commander of soldiers. Vanguard of Faith. Simple trusting, never doubting, knowing it in your bones kinda confidence is the epitome of God's desire for us. Blessed Assurance is a wonderful song. It is a song by Fanny Crosby, one of America's most prolific hymn writers; she wrote over 8,000 Gospel songs and hymns during her 95 years. All of her days, except the first six weeks, were spent in blindness but she chose faith over pain and wrote. Her repertoire includes 1,000+ nonreligious songs, four books of poetry and two best-selling autobiographies published but today her Faith is what carries her. She is in Glory because of her Blessed Assurance. The Commander didn't earn the healing for his servant, He believed for the healing. Often we get caught up in the actions instead of the persuasion of our faith. We believe we must walk it out but simple trust is worthless yet Jesus told this man he would go with Him to heal the servant and the Commander said, no need...just say the words and it will be done. This faith, simple trust and complete confidence is what Jesus desires, commented on and needs from us. There is a saying that faith isn't faith until it is all you are clinging to...I will change it. Faith is Vanguard Faith when the situation looks impossible but He is all you are trusting. He is our all in all. He is our source, our strength, our Prince of Peace, Mighty God, Counselor, Shepherd, Lion of Judah and the list goes on. Most of all, He is our Vanguard of Faith. He is our Faith. Faith is an action. I Faith God. I Trust God with all I am and all I will ever be. "Have Faith in God" isn't a strong enough statement. I Faith God. I (Fully Affirm In The Holiest of Holy!) I Faith! I do not want to be the outside to grace, the one who grew up in the faith but abandoned faith. I want to be the one who pours in from the west and sits down at God's banquet table with the pillars of faith. I Fully Affirm In The Holiest! I Faith!

Jesus, overhearing, shot back, "Who needs a doctor: the healthy or the sick? Go figure out what this Scripture means: 'I'm after mercy, not religion.' I'm here to invite outsiders, not coddle insiders."

Just then a woman who had hemorrhaged for twelve years slipped in from behind and lightly touched his robe. She was thinking to herself, "If I can just put a finger on his robe, I'll get well." Jesus turned—caught her at it. Then he reassured her: "Courage, daughter. You took a risk of faith, and now you're well." The woman was well from then on.

Matthew 9: 12-13, 20-22

Whole!

Who needs Jesus? We all do but some of us see the need and others do not. I tend to go to the doctor more quickly than my boys and spouse. They tend to tough it out. If I need help or have problems, I tend to turn to resources and get help by asking rather than trying to rough it. This includes asking directions, getting assistance and requesting prayer but most importantly it means I seek God first and foremost. In these verses in Matthew, Jesus was being ridiculed and put down by the religious leaders of the day for association with the common people. He responded by asking them who needed the help, the sick or the well? The truth is many people don't know they are sick and need a doctor until it is later and the same is with Christ. Many people celebrate the holidays around His birth and resurrection as Santa and the Easter Bunny never understanding the true meaning. I have read and seen so many incorrect depictions because people fail to realize the need inside them. In this story, a lady weak with loss of blood and cast out from the crowd due to her "uncleanness" courageously and boldly took a step in His direction to brush the hem of His garment. It wasn't the touch of His clothing that healed her, it was her faith. Jesus told her this. It was that she stretched out to Him in her great need and knew in her heart and mind that touching Jesus was all that mattered-that her life would never be the old wreck it was and that it would change/heal/restore her. We need to get to that place of desperation where touching Jesus is all that matters. We need to begin to look At our lives through His eyes and see our own brokenness and weaknesses. He is our source-there is no other. Jesus didn't come to be the star of a show-He is already the creator of the stars. He didn't come for wealth and fame as He already had all He needed or wanted in those areas. He came to the lowliest and poor to demonstrate that He is about those in need. Your wealth, ability and strengths do not determine your status with Jesus. Your words, talents and skills do not matter to Jesus. You are His child and when you hurt, He only wants to touch you and make you whole. Wholeness isn't just about healing. Wholeness is about Holy boldness and courage to take the steps. Wholeness is trusting when the way is dark and unclear. Wholeness is complete contentment in who He is despite the circumstances that surround you. If we can just touch Him in Faith believing, we will be made whole. What is whole? Covered in mercy, filled with His grace and healed from our own expectations of perfection is what wholeness means. Lord I believe, but help my unbelief. Recognize the doubt that exists; acknowledge it and repent of it so He can move miraculously in you. The miracle of the seasons isn't the birth or death of Christ although those are mighty things. The miracle is the restoration to Life. Jesus is the Way, Truth and Life. Restoration to Him through His merciful sacrifice is available for all who will. The work was done on the cross when Jesus declared "It is Finished". The battle is over! The victory is won. We just have to step out onto the field of victory with Jesus as our champion. It is the step of faith that leads to wholeness: whatever that gap is that needs to be filled, take it to Jesus.

"If you don't go all the way with me, through thick and thin, you don't deserve me. If your first concern is to look after yourself, you'll never find yourself. But if you forget about yourself and look to me, you'll find both yourself and me.

Matthew 10: 38-39

Salinity!

In this photo it looks like two different places but it's actually the same body of water. The difference is that the salinity of the water that is pink is ten times that of the ocean as the salt flats feed into it but just over the road, this part of the water is refreshed by three different rivers of fresh water that keeps the salt content negligible. Jesus compares us to salt in this world. Salt is a valuable commodity but too much of it makes it indigestible and poisonous for the body. Too little of salt and the preservative quality is lost and just a hint gives flavor but no change. In Matthew, Jesus admonishes us that if we are not willing to go all the way with Him through thick and thin, we don't deserve Him. If we focus first on ourselves and not on Him, then our saltiness is lost. If we focus on Him and forget about ourselves, looking only to Him, we will find Him and ourselves. He is saying to us to allow Him to carry the details. We just mess things up when He has a way. Today is a day of celebration of life. Today is an opportunity to rectify the selfish way and turn it over to Him. Today is a day to dive deep into His saltiness and allow Him to preserve us into the persons He wants us to be. We must get past the worry of being too salty for He is the Living Water that provides the balance. We must get past the concepts that the church, the Christ walk cannot stand up for fear of being too salty. We must quit watering down the gospel message with the tainted waters of the world and turn once again into His ways. It may not be the popular way, but it's the right way. It may not seem to be the right way, but if we focus on Him, He will balance the Salt, The Light and The Living Water into the right balance of delivery and life. Immersion in Him is the right way. Resurrection is about life after death. Jesus is the Resurrection and the Life which no man can bypass to the Father as He is the only Way. Don't hold back, dive into His grace.

"How can I account for this generation? The people have been like spoiled children whining to their parents, 'We wanted to skip rope, and you were always too tired; we wanted to talk, but you were always too busy.' John came fasting and they called him crazy. I came feasting and they called me a boozer, a friend of the misfits. Opinion polls don't count for much, do they? The proof of the pudding is in the eating."

Matthew 11: 16-19

Proof!

Thomas was called Doubting Thomas because he said he wouldn't believe Jesus had risen until he touched His nail scarred hands and His scarred side. Thomas was called Doubting...what are we called? Jesus asked how He could account for this generation...calling them spoiled, whiny children without a clue as to who He was....what should we be called? In all other Bible versions, the last part of this verse says Wisdom is justified or proved right by her deeds...proof! It can look good, sound good and be told about, that it is good but the taste test is what matters. The saying "the proof of the pudding is in the eating" means it doesn't matter what is reported by the news media if you can tell it by the taste. We are daily sold a bill of goods by social media and the local/national news. Some of it is accurate and some is completely skewed by politicians and those in charge. We know as we experience and this is the world Thomas was working in and living in. He had walked with Jesus, seen the miracles and knew Him to be the Son of God but when He was crucified, his hopes were dashed and suddenly all he thought he knew was cast in doubt. This happens to us too. We begin our walk with Jesus. We believe and we see and then the storms come-they are black and ominous. They destroy things we cherished and hopes that we had. They tarnish our beliefs and shake our foundations so that we begin to question who He is. This is the fight of death, hell and the grave. We get upside down with God about why He allows these things. We begin to battle the doubt through our fears without the weapons He provided and that fear, doubt and unbelief begins to choke us. When miracles come, we doubt them. When people report on God's move across the country, we argue on whether it is Him or not. When the situation before us looks impossible, we lose hope. This is the battle that Jesus already fought and won. We are not defeated. We are not lost. The proof of Him isn't in us being at His resurrection or walking into that empty tomb although I have been told it is a humbling and amazing experience. The proof of Him is already done. The battle of the cross was fought in Gethsemane when Jesus accepted His Father's will over His own. The battle on the cross was an accomplishment of that war that had been waged. When Jesus said, "It is Finished", He was done with the flesh and moved into the Spirit. He said "Father, unto you, I commit my Spirit" meaning that I am now leaving this fleshly body. He knew His mortal body would physically be raised and He would inhabit it again for a bit but the war had already been won. The Devil thought the battle was over too and he perceived that he had won so Jesus had to go to Hell and the Grave to declare victory there also. The Resurrection was a day of deliberation for all those who had lost their hopes. They had given up as they watched Him die on the cross and now they huddled in fear and some anticipation of what would be next. Why are we so easy to give up? Why do we who know who He is whine and cry so much? Why are we so opinion driven and short sighted in our faith vision? Because we are spoiled and whiny. Who are we keeping company with? Did we give up the Master for the other servants and now we doubt the Master? There are many days that I can be called Doubting Donesa because like so many others, I get my eyes on my circumstances. I let my hopes of this life dash my hopes of a future like a hailstorm beating at a crop. I fail to recognize the Who He is and get caught up in the What happened. The "what" isn't our future. We wanted....when what we wanted gets dashed, we give up and get discouraged but the truth is that if what we wanted was anchored in the "Who He is", then all our hope would be realized. Opinion polls don't matter. What we see, feel and experience doesn't matter to the Who He is. He has always been and always will be and He is there for us. Don't let our circumstances dictate our future. Turn it over to Him.

"There is far more at stake here than religion. If you had any idea what this Scripture meant—'I prefer a flexible heart to an inflexible ritual'—you wouldn't be nitpicking like this. The Son of Man is no yes-man to the Sabbath; he's in charge."

"You have minds like a snake pit! How do you suppose what you say is worth anything when you are so foul-minded? It's your heart, not the dictionary, that gives meaning to your words. A good person produces good deeds and words season after season. An evil person is a blight on the orchard. Let me tell you something: Every one of these careless words is going to come back to haunt you. There will be a time of Reckoning. Words are powerful; take them seriously. Words can be your salvation. Words can also be your damnation."

Matthew 12: 6-8, 34-37

Reckoning!

The preview. The warning. The forecast. In Matthew 12, Jesus is being harassed by the "church" crowd-the religious right as they try to inject their opinions and ways upon Him but He tells them that God prefers a flexible heart to the legalism. Many have taken this scripture to justify their own way of living outside the laws of God. When Jesus heals on the Sabbath, the religious leaders are infuriated and Jesus charges them with having the minds of a snake. In verse 43-45, Jesus cautions that cleaning the house of wicked ways but not allowing Christ to inhabit freely just allows more of the devil and his minions to inhabit-7 times as many as before Salvation. This clearly indicates that salvation is not a singular action but a process of redemption in relationship. A storm warmed area receives an alert that a storm could be coming but often the storm itself arrives unexpectedly and off in timing. Jesus is our lighthouse, warning us that the shores of danger are close and our ship is sailing through the storm too close to the rough spots. He says our words can be our salvation or damnation all by the intent of our heart. I will never forget when John was in first grade and this truth was made clear. You see, my boys hadn't heard any foul language and I always told them people who used curse words lacked adequacy in their vocabulary, so they resorted to gutter language. The teacher called me to explain that they were discussing careers and that John had told the class his dad was a game warden who had gone down to New Orleans to assist the people being flooded out by the "dam thing". The class all laughed and hooted and hollered as they lacked vocabulary, and so thought he had cursed. The teacher told me she had handled it in class but wanted me to explain to John that dam was a homonym for damn and so not to use that word. I told her no. I was not going to limit my son's ability to learn and grow by the limitations of others' expectations and vocabulary. John has learned what both words mean now as he is grown much to my chagrin. The point is that words have power and intent. This intent and meaning come from the heart and the mind. If you fix your heart and mind on God, then your words should follow that pattern. Careless words lead to a day of reckoning! Be wise with your word choices and true to the character that God places in you when you dwell in Him.

While he was still talking to the crowd, his mother and brothers showed up. They were outside trying to get a message to him. Someone told Jesus, "Your mother and brothers are out here, wanting to speak with you."

Jesus didn't respond directly, but said, "Who do you think my mother and brothers are?" He then stretched out his hand toward his disciples. "Look closely. These are my mother and brothers. Obedience is thicker than blood. The person who obeys my heavenly Father's will is my brother and sister and mother."

Matthew 12: 46-50

Obedience!

Obedience isn't agreement. Obedience isn't acquiescence. Obedience isn't rebellion. Obedience isn't questioning why. The definition of obedience is compliance with an order, request, or law or submission to another's authority. Jesus equates obedience with closeness and connection and relationship when He says in Matthew that obedience is thicker than blood. He clearly identifies that through obedience we become His family in relationship with Him. Obedience to our Father's will is the way to open the doors of Heaven into our lives. Submission is a word that has become foreign to our society just like obedience. In fact, the fastest growing learning issue right now is oppositional defiance disorder which is rebellious behavior where the brain is caught in fight or flight. While experts struggle to define the reasoning behind the rapid growth of this disorder in the brain, the Bible tells us that it is the spiritual equivalent of rebelliousness. Family is an important and integral part of who we are and often they force us into decisions and actions we wouldn't normally take because we prioritize them. I am not saying this is wrong but rather saying that our actions and words need to align with God first then family. If family loyalty is bringing you to a place of violation of God's law and principles, then a decision must be made which is often difficult for whom you will serve. I dearly love my family and I chuckle as my dad's siblings banter on our group text messages. They are a tough teasing crowd and they love one another dearly. They have been through many tough times together but the truth is that they too must make the same decisions we all do which is often hard. Whom will we serve? Will we choose to be a part of the family of God not because we are blood bought but because we choose to serve His will obediently?

He replied, "You've been given insight into God's kingdom. You know how it works. Not everybody has this gift, this insight; it hasn't been given to them. Whenever someone has a ready heart for this, the insights and understandings flow freely. But if there is no readiness, any trace of receptivity soon disappears. That's why I tell stories: to create readiness, to nudge the people toward a welcome awakening. In their present state they can stare till doomsday and not see it, listen till they're blue in the face and not get it. I don't want Isaiah's forecast repeated all over again: Your ears are open but you don't hear a thing.
Your eyes are awake but you don't see a thing.
The people are stupid! They stick their fingers in their ears so they won't have to listen;They screw their eyes shut so they won't have to look,so they won't have to deal with me face-to-faceand let me heal them.
"But you have God-blessed eyes—eyes that see! And God-blessed ears—ears that hear! A lot of people, prophets and humble believers among them, would have given anything to see what you are seeing, to hear what you are hearing, but never had the chance.

Matthew 13: 11-17

Receptivity!

Whenever it rains, my tv and satellite system gets all jammed up and cannot read the signal so reception is spotty and inconsistent. Often this affects the internet and other means of communication too such as cellphones. In life, when storms come our way, often our reception to God's plan and will in our lives feels the same way. In Matthew 13, Jesus is explaining Himself to his closest disciples as they have questioned why He keeps telling the same type of stories about farmers and planting in relation to what He is communicating to the people. Jesus patiently explains that those closest to Him have a clearer signal or insight and more understanding of His message while others struggle with having the readiness or willingness to receive the message. The error message I get on my TV will say something like-please remove debris or other things that are obscuring the signal. Often this is the message we need to hear from God too. I work with a lot of struggling learners and when the brain has a hard time receiving the information due to learning delays or cognitive weaknesses, it makes receiving the information very difficult if not impossible for the learner. That weakness can be a listening issue in their auditory processing or a memory issue among others. Whatever the reason, when the learning process is broken down and trained deliberately then there is growth in the receiving. This is what Jesus was explaining to His disciples. When we clear the issue with hearing up and reception is open, the message can be learned, applied and acted upon but when there is confusion, it leads to frustration and an overwhelmed feeling. I hear people say they would give anything to have walked with Jesus but the truth is that walking with Him daily and seeing Him work is much easier today than then because we have His words to guide us written plainly before us. Yet even now, many are like those in this text who figuratively stick their fingers in their ears refusing to hear what God is saying or closing their eyes to the reality of God moving before them by choice. If there is no willingness to clear the debris, open the ears to hear and the eyes to see Him at work, then the reception to His message is lost and the time is wasted. A recent hailstorm beat down upon our home and this was one of over twenty hailstorms in the last three years at our home. This storm did damage to many things but our insurance company is once again in a place of denial despite evidence via photos, videos, multiple roofers testimonies, etc. They are completely sticking their fingers in their ears and covering their eyes to reality because there is a cost to them if they recognize the truth. This is the reality for many of us. We do not want to hear or see what God is saying to us because the cost is more than we are willing to bear. We are not receptive to His words, will and message. We do not make the time to prioritize Him but rather put Him on a back burner. Jesus said, in their present state...they can stare until doomsday and not see, listen until they are blue in the face and not get it because their hearts are not open to see/hear what He is saying. When a child doesn't want to hear correction, they often turn away, stick fingers in ears or close eyes because they choose to not receive the correction or message. Many of us are like that too. We tune in readily to the good news and our rewards, but when the message requires us to read, focus and act, we would rather stick our fingers in our ears to block receiving than to be faced with the truth which requires us to be responsible for the message. They would rather sit in misery and sickness than to accept the truth and be healed. A ready heart that is receptive to what God is saying and doing, flows freely in understanding and insights into His will and way but even the person who has a willing heart must keep the debris cleared or reception becomes spotty. How's your signal? Do you need to clear some debris or perhaps take blinders off or remove your fingers from your ears? Is God speaking to you but you are choosing to play stupid and ignore His plain message? Do you need story time to make His message more clear? God blessed eyes and ears are those that are clear of debris and ready to receive. If you are wanting to receive the blessings of God, get to clearing the debris that is causing the receptivity issue. Loud and clear, the signs of the times scream Jesus is coming very soon. In order to be ready to hear that trumpet sound, we need a clear signal to receive and hear/see what He is saying. Prepare your own heart so that you might be blessed.

So he explained. "The farmer who sows the pure seed is the Son of Man. The field is the world, the pure seeds are subjects of the kingdom, the thistles are subjects of the Devil, and the enemy who sows them is the Devil. The harvest is the end of the age, the curtain of history. The harvest hands are angels.

"The picture of thistles pulled up and burned is a scene from the final act. The Son of Man will send his angels, weed out the thistles from his kingdom, pitch them in the trash, and be done with them. They are going to complain to high heaven, but nobody is going to listen. At the same time, ripe, holy lives will mature and adorn the kingdom of their Father.

"Are you listening to this? Really listening?

Jesus asked, "Are you starting to get a handle on all this?"
They answered, "Yes."
He said, "Then you see how every student well-trained in God's kingdom is like the owner of a general store who can put his hands on anything you need, old or new, exactly when you need it."

Matthew 13: 37-43, 51-52

Curtains!

I have been going a little crazy lately, because the curtains got knocked down at my house that go across the top of my drapes. Every time I look at it, it irritates me because it's not right. I can't correct the look myself because I can't stand on the ladder or use a tool to reach it to correct it and the people around me do not see it as a priority. As the sun goes down and sets across the beautiful water, it looks like a beautiful curtain closing on a special scene each night. In Matthew chapter 13 Jesus is telling a parable about a farmer sowing the seeds, and then he explains that the pure seed is Jesus Himself. He also explains that the field is the world, and the seeds are those of us who accept his teachings. He explains that there were thistles that are sown in by the devil, who are the evil people in the world, and the harvest hands are the Angels. At the end of time, the Angels will pull up the thistles, and bind them together, and burn them in the pit of hell with the devil himself. I think of this life as a play with beautiful scenery and characters of both good and bad. The story Jesus tells in this parable is all about the story of life. And he explains that we are the seeds which ripen into harvest and the Angels weed the evil ones from us. Then Jesus asked, are you listening? Are you starting to get a handle on this? really listening? The reason he poses this question is because we get so distracted by the thistles, and the evil that is in the world sown by Satan himself, instead of concentrating on our own growth, so that we can be a part of the harvest. Our job is not to get caught up in the day to day and the evil of others and the frustrations. Our job is to grow and produce crops. Our job is to prepare for the harvest. Our job is to do our part in the beautiful story of life, without worrying about what others are doing. When his story is over as a play on the stage, the curtains are closed. As I look at this curtain in my living room, I think of the curtain of life. One day soon, Jesus will come again and the curtains of this world will be forever closed. He will catch his bride away, and the story will live on behind the curtains of this world as a glorious story. Many of us wonder what happily ever after really means, I mean, Cinderella married the prince, and lived happily ever after. Happily ever after is what happens when the curtain closes. The curtains of life are sure. They will close for each of us either with our death to this life or with the coming of Jesus. The closing of the scene is certain and the curtains will come down. What will happen on the other side of the curtains is also certain. We have a choice. We get to choose what happens on the other side of the curtains. Jesus tells us in this parable what happens. Either we are harvested and taken away as his bride to be fruitful in His Kingdom, or we are gathered as tares/thistles by the angels and burn forever in a lake of fire. What we choose on this side of the curtain while this play of life is ongoing determines the course once the curtain closes.

Peter, suddenly bold, said, "Master, if it's really you, call me to come to you on the water." He said, "Come ahead." Jumping out of the boat, Peter walked on the water to Jesus. But when he looked down at the waves churning beneath his feet, he lost his nerve and started to sink. He cried, "Master, save me!" Jesus didn't hesitate. He reached down and grabbed his hand. Then he said, "Faint-heart, what got into you?"

Matthew 14: 28-31

Saved!

Sudden boldness to sudden fear! In this chapter of Matthew, Jesus is saddened by the loss of His cousin John through Herod's nastiness. He tries to slip away and mourn although He knows John is at peace and rest. His earthly emotions are troubled by the grief and the people see Him. Jesus has compassion on them and begins teaching and healing through His own grief. But after a while, the people are hungry so Jesus blesses a small lunch for one into a feast for thousands. Now as Jesus dismisses them, since he placed their needs first, He intends to find a quiet place alone to pray through His grief. He tells the disciples to go to the other side of the water in the boat. Jesus climbs the mountain alone praying all night then a storm comes along and the boat is rocking and the disciples are scared. Suddenly they see a figure on the water coming towards them. It looks to them like a spirit or a ghost at 4am after being in this storm, but it is Jesus and He tells them to not be afraid. Suddenly Peter gets a holy boldness and this is where the text picks up. The storm is still happening but Peter is looking and listening to Jesus so he feels that he can conquer the world as he steps out to walk on the water to Christ. I can imagine the feeling of excitement and trepidation at the same time. He walked on the water all the way to Christ. But as he walks on that water, he feels the pressure and the splashes of water which causes him to look at his circumstances rather than his Savior. The Word says he lost his nerve. The holy boldness evaporated in the reality of the waves because he started doubting. When he realizes his condition, he cries out to Jesus-Master, save me! Jesus reached down and rescued him asking, "Faint-heart, what got into you?"

I so, relate. Just when we are walking in confidence, trusting God to do as He said He would, the waves of life get choppy and splash us reminding us of the cares of this life. Suddenly our minds move from being fixed on the eternal to becoming fixated on the waves of our storm. Our heart loses the nerve because we begin to allow the fear of our circumstances to steal our excitement and joy of His presence. We begin questioning our walk and the Holy Boldness that allows us to conquer fear is suddenly shoved aside by the reality of our circumstances. I just imagine the moment that the Holy boldness of trusting God became a fleshly "look at me, I got this" confidence, was when he looked down. Instead of staying fixed in his mind on Christ. Now all the other disciples watched this. They saw Peter walking on the water to Christ and the two of them walking back. They had seen miracle after miracle but as Jesus climbed into the boat, the storm stopped and this is the point they say, this is it...you really are God. How often do we say we will trust and believe? We see miracles and experience them daily in our own lives but fail to recognize them. We get caught up in the daily grind, and our Holy boldness and assurance that allows us to walk on the waters of life gets all tangled up in our circumstances. Instead of us claiming the victory, we get stuck in the muck and then we cry out for Jesus to rescue us. None of us are immune to this. We are flesh but we have a Savior who was tempted at all points as we are and He proved that He has the power. Instead of looking down in fear at your current financial circumstances or your health or your relationships struggling., call out, reach out to Him. Claim His words. Speak His name over everything from that car battery that won't seem to work to that frustration with the circumstances of your situation. Claim victory in Jesus' name and go conquer those waves. Walk out in Holy boldness to the Savior for He is there calling us to come to Him.

He then called the crowd together and said, "Listen, and take this to heart. It's not what you swallow that pollutes your life, but what you vomit up."

Jesus shrugged it off. "Every tree that wasn't planted by my Father in heaven will be pulled up by its roots. Forget them. They are blind men leading blind men. When a blind man leads a blind man, they both end up in the ditch."

Jesus replied, "You, too? Are you being willfully stupid? Don't you know that anything that is swallowed works its way through the intestines and is finally defecated? But what comes out of the mouth gets its start in the heart. It's from the heart that we vomit up evil arguments, murders, adulteries, fornications, thefts, lies, and cussing. That's what pollutes. Eating or not eating certain foods, washing or not washing your hands—that's neither here nor there."

Matthew 15: 10-11, 13-14, 16-20

Pollution!

Stomach bugs and food poisoning have been an irritating factor of life for several people around me lately but since I have always had a struggle with a sensitive stomach, I understand. I honestly had to read this several times in various versions of scripture to totally grasp what Jesus was saying at deeper than a surface level. Jesus wasn't degrading the law nor putting down the work of justification but rather showing that it is all about what we do with what we are given/dealt/dumped into that matters. What comes from someone's mouth starts in their heart. The pollution of our life starts with the choices we make to allow it to take root in us. People can dump things on us but we have the choice to let it pass on through or over without allowing it to become reactive. When Jesus made these statements, He was being accosted and accused by the religious leaders of that day. Pollution is a catch phrase nowadays for things that defile. Opinions are everywhere on what is good for us or bad for us. The truth is that we have a choice no matter what others say or do. Rule following because someone says or insists we do isn't the way. If you follow a rule with no heart, you are just an actor or performer without a care. If we say it came from our heart. We may regret spewing it out but it is in there and must be worked on. When my boys were little I would discourage them from foul language. My mother in law told me a story that my husband used to have an imaginary friend who cussed so he could get away with saying words she didn't allow. He would tell her that his friend said such and such...sometimes we all have these imaginary or false people in our lives. The alter ego, counterpart to our souls that flares up and spews out evil which harbored within us and grew. The actions and reactions we give to life are because we allow the heart to harbor the things not of God. We need to become HeartSmart so that we can HeartStart in God's will rather than being a HeartFart in our words and actions to others.

"And that's not all. You will have complete and free access to God's kingdom, keys to open any and every door: no more barriers between heaven and earth, earth and heaven. A yes on earth is yes in heaven. A no on earth is no in heaven."

"Don't be in such a hurry to go into business for yourself. Before you know it the Son of Man will arrive with all the splendor of his Father, accompanied by an army of angels. You'll get everything you have coming to you, a personal gift. This isn't pie in the sky by and by. Some of you standing here are going to see it take place, see the Son of Man in kingdom glory."

Matthew 16: 19, 27-28

Access!

Passwords, keys, remote entry and automatic access are all ways to enter a location or place. We have these through Jesus. He has established free and complete access to God's kingdom through His love and sacrifice if we but believe. As Jesus shared with the disciples in Matthew, it isn't about our own way of business and getting through, that works. His provision is enough. He doesn't want us to just live to get the day over but to live in confidence of who He is in joy that all the barriers between heaven and earth have been removed through Him. What would you do if you had access to all of the money, all the power, and all of the means that you wanted? Would you use it to draw more people to Jesus or would it lead you in a path where you were focused on something other than Him? I hear people say all the time if only I had, if only I could do, if only....my question is, so what are you doing with what you have now? Are you using all of your resources to lead others to Jesus now? Trust is what gives us full access. And more and more hackers are out there and available today trying to steal people's identities, homes, money, and resources because they spend their time trying to cheat others instead of working to gain their own. Jesus was well aware of the people who purported to try to do it right, but were cheating. He knew all about religious leaders and scoffers. He knew, and He knows. It isn't about you and it isn't about me. It is all about Him, and what He has done for us in order to give us full access to all of the resources that He has, but we must first believe. I see the question that was asked right before this verse... by Jesus... was, Who do they say that I am? The disciples answered that many of the people believed Jesus to be Elijah or other prophets, and then Jesus said, who do you believe that I am? Peter answered I believe you to be the Messiah, the savior of the world. That is the complete and full access to all that Jesus has And will do.

The automatic access to the gate of Heaven requires only one password, Jesus, the key, the way, the truth and light. What is it that you want so bad? What is it that you need access to in order to make you happy? The answer is Jesus. He is the answer. People are searching the world over, trying to find happiness that can only be found through Him. Happiness all the time and wonderful peace of mind is found through Jesus. Here I am Lord. All I have is yours if you will have all of me. Use me today throughout my pain and my lack to shine joy into the hearts of others. Let me be enriched with your light so that others may know and be blessed.

While he was going on like this, babbling, a light-radiant cloud enveloped them, and sounding from deep in the cloud a voice: "This is my Son, marked by my love, focus of my delight. Listen to him."

Jesus said, "What a generation! No sense of God! No focus to your lives! How many times do I have to go over these things? How much longer do I have to put up with this? Bring the boy here." He ordered the afflicting demon out—and it was out, gone. From that moment on the boy was well.

"Because you're not yet taking God seriously," said Jesus. "The simple truth is that if you had a mere kernel of faith, a poppy seed, say, you would tell this mountain, 'Move!' and it would move. There is nothing you wouldn't be able to tackle."

Matthew 17: 5, 17-18, 20

Move!

Photos are moments frozen in time, captured memory, a precious reflection and a simple portrait of a singular second. Yet a picture of words or visual imagery can say many things. This photo captures the moment after a storm where all is quiet in relief but to others it speaks something altogether different. The perception is in the focus. Jesus was transfigured on the Mount before the disciples and they heard God speak over Him not just this once but for the second time. Even then, they struggled with belief in who He is, was and will forever be. Jesus seems very frustrated as He comments on the generation with no focus. My sons have often gotten irritated that people make negative comments about their generation lacking in certain ways but God saw this lack in many generations before them. We struggle with belief and we anticipate failure in all we do rather than having complete confidence. A childlike faith is one that believes no matter what the circumstances dictate otherwise. I understand disappointment and I understand Jesus' frustration because I know He feels it with me when I struggle to call things as they are spiritually rather than how they are seen in the flesh. Many seeds I plant but few I expect to germinate and be fruitful rather than expecting all. Why? As a child, we are easily captivated by the promise and we live for the reward. Then one time we are disappointed and we let that begin to write into us a seed of doubt, distrust and unbelief. The same happens to the spiritual child in us. We believe then things don't turn out how we expected, we sow a seed of distrust and unbelief into our fertile soul soil. What is it about weeds that they always germinate? Perhaps it is our focus. When we get angry or disappointed in a circumstance or situation that God allowed, unlike Job, we become disillusioned and filled with discontent. We nurture the seedling of distrust and the weeds of unbelief. We fail to recognize the promise and focus on the now vision. What would happen if we woke up saying Lord, I believe and acted on it? What would happen if we fertilized the mustard seed of faith daily by speaking the words of life and beauty, watering it with His living water of the word? The simple truth is that we could speak to storms to be still, both physical and emotional, mental, financial, etc. The simple truth is that we could do more, be more, overcome more. The simple truth is that it is all about which seeds we are cultivating in our lives.

But the Lord is faithful, who will establish you and guard you from the evil one. And we have confidence in the Lord concerning you, both that you do and will do the things we command you.
Now may the Lord direct your hearts into the love of God and into the patience of Christ.

2 Thessalonians 3: 3-5

Established!

I have no idea how old this tree in this picture is. You can only see one portion of it due to its established nature. I saw two pictures of it taken 125 years apart and it had spread much wider although it looked a little lighter in some of the branches. I imagine that it also had seen a lot of things, had a lot of burdens, harbored a lot of life and endured many storms. This tree probably lost branches and had many things happen to it from ice storms to high winds and heat but it has continued despite all hardship to grow and thrive. Not all trees do. What establishes us when the going gets tough? The faithfulness of God directing us in love into the patience of Christ. If you think Jesus had an easy time of it here on Earth, you aren't reading the same words I do. If you think any of the people in scripture had an easy time....life is hard and it isn't fair but God is faithful. One of my favorite songs is "I've been through enough to know He'll be enough for me. He's come through too many times which puts my heart at ease for good. I'll stake my very life that He's going to take care of me. For I have been through enough to know He will be enough for me." What directs our hearts into patience? Trials, storms, hardships...most people don't realize this but the hardship on the tree when it is established isn't the same thing as when it was a sapling. Establishing means rooting deeply. A tree that never experienced hardship as a sapling will not establish deeply. If the roots don't dig in deep seeking the source of water deep in the earth, then when tough times of drought or high winds come, it will not be able to withstand. Even if a tree becomes established but stops growing, it will soon pull away from its own roots and die whether due to parasites or vines or other. We cause a lot of our own issues because we do not faithfully seek Him in continued growth during tough circumstances. We give up. We fail to see His promises and provisions, instead looking at and becoming overwhelmed with the things eating away at our bark, the woodpeckers, the vines, the termites, etc. We have a choice to grow in Him, digging deeper and becoming more rooted or to simply give it up and lay down. We may age, become lean, missing a few parts or losing vision, hair, teeth and other muscle tone but we do not have to lay down...instead we should lay it down. Let the branches of our lives grow a little wider. Spread a little more, root a little deeper in the confidence that He is able and He will keep you. Stay rooted and established in His love and grace. Trust His direction. It may not look like you thought it would, but if you trust Him, He is faithful and He will guard you and direct you.

For an answer Jesus called over a child, whom he stood in the middle of the room, and said, "I'm telling you, once and for all, that unless you return to square one and start over like children, you're not even going to get a look at the kingdom, let alone get in. Whoever becomes simple and elemental again, like this child, will rank high in God's kingdom. What's more, when you receive the childlike on my account, it's the same as receiving me.

"But if you give them a hard time, bullying or taking advantage of their simple trust, you'll soon wish you hadn't. You'd be better off dropped in the middle of the lake with a millstone around your neck. Doom to the world for giving these God-believing children a hard time! Hard times are inevitable, but you don't have to make it worse— and it's doomsday to you if you do.

Matthew 18: 2-7

Elemental!

If you look closely at this photo of a field of flowers, right where it says "make it" you will see among the orange poppies, there is a purple lavender blooming. It is unique and elemental in its growth. I can imagine that flower struggling in the field of others being different and unique. Different and unique is what we are called to be. Simply as He made us. No pretense or change. No need to be something more. Just be the You He designed you to be! Know Him and Be You!

Simple and elemental means getting back to the basics of life without all the complications. It is a place of being rooted in who you are no matter what everyone else thinks or says. Jesus says in Matthew that bullying or taking advantage of the simple minded or those with innate trust in Him is a death sentence. He says Doom to the world and all those who give God-believing children a hard time. A lot of people struggle with belief as it is due to all the world's ways but if we complicate it and make it more so, Jesus says it is worse for us. You see, there are many speakers and preachers who preach Jesus on a national stage and we do not all agree on principles but Jesus has already said that if they preach Him to leave them alone because it becomes confusing to young Christians and young ones. We have had a mass moving away from the gospel and the church just because of this very thing. Let me be clear: preaching the truth is the truth but if it goes against scripture/ that isn't truth. The confusion is in what is the truth. Jesus is The Way, The Truth and The Life. If it aligns with Him, leave them alone. But if it is confusing or directly teaching against the Godly truths recorded, then it isn't truth. Elemental compounds are the combining of two things. When this happens, they are no longer elemental. Basic truth is what Jesus says. Basic faith, very simple, very plain and quite clear. God says it, I believe it. That settles it. No confusion. Just straight truth.

He is who He says He is. It's Elemental!

"Take this most seriously: A yes on earth is yes in heaven; a no on earth is no in heaven. What you say to one another is eternal. I mean this. When two of you get together on anything at all on earth and make a prayer of it, my Father in heaven goes into action. And when two or three of you are together because of me, you can be sure that I'll be there."

Matthew 18: 18-20

Centered!

   Our words have power. What we say to ourselves matters and what we put out into our environment matters but mostly we must realize that the words we speak bring life or death to our spiritual walk. When we walk in continuity with Christ, centered and focused on Him, our life flourishes because we are speaking life, walking in joy and surrendered to His blessings but when we allow disappointments to rain on us so we get soaked in their storms but refuse to dry out in His Son...then we become very beat down and negative. This negativity is like walking around in mucky wet ground in wet clothes...staying in the mud by choice. When the storms of life seem constant and unpredictable, never giving us relief, then we begin to give up ever drying out so that we start speaking negatively in all we do and feeling overwhelmed. Jesus tells us in Matthew's gospel that we should take our words most seriously because they have power. We accept that when we walk across a field of flowers, some of them will be trampled underfoot because we understand the impact of our walk and weight upon the fragility of the flower but have we considered the weight of our words upon the fragility of this earth. What we speak matters because God has given power and authority to our words. The God who said, Let there be Light and caused the Sun, moon and stars to form by His words, says to us that our yes on earth is a yes in Heaven and a no on earth is a no in Heaven. When we pray in agreement on anything, it forces action in Heaven. And when we are together in Him, He is with us. We must quit walking in the storm clouds constantly being buffeted about by the storm and speak the words of life instead. The PeaceSpeaker knows us by name. We have His power through the name of Jesus to stop the storms. We have that power. Picture our breaths and what our breath alone does to a dandelion. It spreads the seeds far and wide. Our words spread life or death to those around us. Our words can alter our situation by speaking life through trust in Him no matter what the storm rains down or like all those who surrounded Job, our words can speak death and disappointment, anger, hate, disbelief, etc. Our words have power. Our words come from the abundance of our heart. Do we trust God? Speak His words of truth. What we say to one another is eternal. Jesus said so and even reiterated it with "I mean this." Are we speaking negatively into our situation or are we speaking life? Are our words casting life or death to our dreams, our family, our mission-fields of ministry? One of my favorite songs says-Wonderful words of life and beauty teach us faith and duty...beautiful words, wonderful words, wonderful words of life. Speak His truth over our situations and watch things begin to spring back to life.

But Jesus said, "Not everyone is mature enough to live a married life. It requires a certain aptitude and grace. Marriage isn't for everyone. Some, from birth seemingly, never give marriage a thought. Others never get asked—or accepted. And some decide not to get married for kingdom reasons. But if you're capable of growing into the largeness of marriage, do it."

Matthew 19: 11-12

Largeness!

Recently, a young man who has been married about six months stopped by the house and I asked him about married life. He said he had gained ten pounds and I told him that was called the honeymoon honeybun. We laughed then this morning I chuckled as I read what Jesus said in Matthew about being capable of growing into the largeness of marriage! I am sure He wasn't meaning weight but rather the challenges that marriage itself introduces in life. As Jesus discusses the sacredness of marriage in response to questions about divorce, He reiterates that the challenge of joining two sexes/genders into one person in marriage is permanent and that it shouldn't be allowed to dissolve. We have a culture that is focused on sexuality and marriage as a day to day decision rather than a lifetime commitment. We have a culture focused on lifestyle and how they feel in the moment rather than the hardships that come in choosing marriage. Marriage isn't for the timid. Jesus says not everyone is mature enough to live a married life. It requires a certain aptitude and grace. In the culture of that day, marriage was the lifestyle and it was lifelong, mostly arranged and without choice by the women. What strikes me here is that Jesus, the Son of the Living God deemed marriage as not only a sacred bond between man and woman as God designed it but also as a bond that is never broken even though some had allowed it to be broken by law at that time. Cultural shift has marriage as a shoe to try on and wear a while then discard when it doesn't fit right or is uncomfortable. There are many who commit to marriage wholeheartedly but the spouse isn't as committed or allows the temptations of life to draw them into adultery which breaks the marriage vow. When reading scripture, I see the discrepancy on how marriage was as a cultural fixture and how Jesus perceived it very differently. You see Jesus sees marriage from the viewpoint of the Prince looking at His princess bride as a precious pearl of great price. Jesus sees marriage as a commitment that is forever, eternal and a growing together. My staff and I visited the American Rose Center not too long ago and we saw the hybrid roses that had morphed from two bushes side by side beginning to share genetic materials so that a new breed of rose was born. A bush completely covered in red roses with a single light yellowish pink beauty because of the marriage between that bush and the one next to it which was a vibrant gold. That newness of life is marriage. When a man/woman choose to become one flesh, it isn't only a physical act but it is spiritual in nature. A bond that cannot be broken. When a marriage is legally broken, it doesn't erase that bond. Forever there will be memories and thoughts, feelings and emotions that pertain only to that bond. Sexual intimacy changes the brain chemistry permanently. The intimacy releases hormones never previously released and changes the brain's chemistry. Lots of research and data out there on how marriage and sexual intimacy change the brain but Jesus called it growing into the largeness of marriage. Why? Because marriage requires largesse, the complete open generosity of giving of oneself sometimes at the expense of oneself. It is a willingness to give with the knowledge that the other person is also willing to lay down their self. So what exactly does this largeness do for us? It grows us, changes us and makes us new. This is why marriage is the comparison that God uses for our relationship with Him! We lay down our own will to submit to His way, knowing that He has our best interests in mind and that all He is doing in us is for the good of our own selves and the marriage relationship with Him. Jesus is the bridegroom who laid down His very life to redeem the bride for eternity. He paid the bride price with His life. He paid the cost of redemption so that no one, male or female is lost. Largeness is the sacrifice of self for the greater good of the new relationship. This means laying down my own dreams and ideas to make new dreams and create fresh ideas with my spouse. It means being willing to lose out on my own ways and my will in favor of togetherness. Marriage isn't for everyone. It requires a certain grace and aptitude. Not just any grace and not just any aptitude but a certain one-a particular one. Aptitude is a suitability or natural ability towards grace-courteous goodwill in all circumstances. Think of that. Marriage requires the willingness to be of a forgiving nature and a willingness to work towards that which isn't natural. Becoming one means leaning into the other and losing the part of self that keeps you from uniting completely. It is work. It is a choice each minute of every day. Some of us have grown in the largeness of marriage on the scale and not in the marriage itself. Perhaps it is time to examine this more fully. Largeness. Choice. Let's stretch ourselves today in our marriages to be a little larger in our love, our forgiveness, our focus, our commitment, our compassion and in our selflessness.

"If you want to give it all you've got," Jesus replied, "go sell your possessions; give everything to the poor. All your wealth will then be in heaven.
Then come follow me."
That was the last thing the young man expected to hear. And so, crestfallen, he walked away. He was holding on tight to a lot of things, and he couldn't bear to let go.

Matthew 19: 21-22

Crestfallen!

Yesterday was a day of divesting myself of things that have held me back in ways I didn't realize. It wasn't a big deal to anyone else, simply a closet clean-out but to me, it was a learning process to let go. In this passage in Matthew, Jesus is speaking with a young man who is a leader in his community, highly sought after and a follower of Christ but as he comes before Jesus asking how he can draw closer, Jesus tells him that if he wants to give it all he's got, trust God with all of it, then he has to let go of the security blanket of his possessions and wealth loved so dearly on this Earth. What a sad moment for him that it was the last thing he expected so he walked away crestfallen. He was holding onto the security of things so tightly that he couldn't let go and trust Jesus. Oh how I relate. We are so bound by our known and our comforts that we truly have no idea how to fully rely on God. As we sorted through things yesterday, I realized how bound I had become by the trappings of this life. Laying up treasures here for myself, my kids, and my future is not a bad thing but it is a type of bondage to feel obligated to hold onto things that have no eternal value. I found the shoes I wore on my wedding day and thought, if only I could tell that young lady as she donned these shoes to let it go. Don't be so uptight with things always turning out right. Let it go and trust God. In the impossible he becomes the I'm possible. In the important, He becomes the I'm portent-the exceptional, the amazing, the wonderful. As I let go of things yesterday, a weight slid off that I didn't even realize was there at all. I became lighter literally and figuratively as many pounds of things were transported away. What is it that you cannot bear to let go of? The letting go is when you ride the wave rather than get towed under it. In this photo, a residual cloud of air disrupted appears in the northern lights as the SpaceX rocket left Earth. Evidence of the rocket breaking free of Earth's bounds appeared in the sky. What is the evidence of us breaking free of the bounds of Earth? Freedom in Jesus... The upper room filled once again with spontaneous prayers and speaking in tongues as the Holy Spirit descended. Let go and let God.

Remember: A stingy planter gets a stingy crop; a lavish planter gets a lavish crop. I want each of you to take plenty of time to think it over, and make up your own mind what you will give. That will protect you against sob stories and arm-twisting. God loves it when the giver delights in the giving.

2 Corinthians 9: 6-7

Lavish!

The beautiful flowers in this picture are planted only by God. They are called wildflowers because God uses the creatures of nature and natural habitat to grow beauty without us but when we want crops to eat, we control the planting, the thinning, the maintenance and the harvesting. In 2 Corinthians, we are reminded that what we sow is what we reap. If we sow the merest little bit in order to just get by into the kingdom of God, then we will reap only the little. If we sow lavishly into His purpose without regret, we will reach a huge harvest but sometimes that harvest pays off later than we see. My parents had 4 children and now have 8 grandchildren even though we lost my brother before he had children, my parents have already seen a double portion. As these grandchildren marry and reproduce, more legacy will be born and what my parents sowed will continue to reproduce long after they see it. Sowing lavishly into our families and our world doesn't mean we have to give up all we have but it does mean that we do not hold back. Sowing can be a financial principle as it is in this scripture. It is a principle of giving in delight and joy rather than in obligation. I am so excited when God blesses us because it allows us to sow more into His kingdom in giving and tithes. Sowing involves more than casting seed upon fertile ground. It involves making the ground ready to receive through consistent work of tilling and clearing. I am not a gardener by nature. I enjoy watching my husband do it and I love getting the crop from his work but I am not able to do all of the physical work it requires. God has called all of us to the mission fields of planting and harvesting though. It doesn't require a lot of physical means always but it does require a willingness to tune into the Master Gardener's directions. He has given us each seed to sow into our own lives and others but it requires us to do the labor. He said if we have faith as a mustard seed, we can say to the mountains to remove themselves into the sea and they would do it. This is the calling He has for each of us. The planting of the mustard seed of faith. Now, why a mustard seed? It is a very tiny seed that produces a huge perpetual crop. But even that tiny seed will be snatched away by birds or baked by the sun if it isn't planted and cared for properly. Faith is the substance of things hoped for and the evidence of things not yet seen. This tiny seed is the potential for growth and the proof that growth can happen but until it is planted, it is only potential. The sowing is the practice. The waiting is the hard part. The trusting is the maintenance and the believing when we cannot see it, is the practice. When we plant in a ready field, and we sow lavishly, then we will have many crops but also many weeds. We will have to continue to care for that growing plant of faith in our lives so that every storm doesn't wash away the soil it is rooted in and water it with the word of living water so that the sun will not bake it to a crisp before it produces. I have watched people who throw out seed onto ground that has never been prepared and somehow, something takes root. It is surprising but it happens. I have watched a farmer carefully tend a field, sow and nourish, then life happens and his crop is wiped out like Job in scripture. But in all my life, no matter what, God has never failed to be faithful to me despite my failures. He has reseeded and grown from the washes of storm in other places where I never expected but He has never failed me. Disappointments-yes, I have had many. But His word was still true. Sorrows, yes, I have had these also. Discouraged days and nights have come without a doubt but His song came too. God loves it when we sow in delight despite our pain and circumstances. He loves when we give it our all just because we can. God loves a cheerful giver because when we give in cheer, it is contagious like laughter. The crop we sow lavishly we will reap lavishly so we can sow in faith that will move mountains or we can sow in doubt that will reproduce bitterness and disease. We can sow in confidence that He is able or we can sow in disappointment that we doubt His favor. What we sow is what we reap. What we say is what we get back. What we give is what we receive. What we send out is what comes back in double portions. It is our choice what to sow. We are all gardeners in our lives. It is our choice to sow with Him in faith and reproduce a legacy of faithfulness or to sow in doubt and get a meager crop of bitter weed. Remember. Lavish sowing gets a lavish harvest but what we sow matters. What are you planting in the lives of others around you?

But you, God, shield me
on all sides;
You ground my feet, you
lift my head high;
With all my might
I shout up to God,
His answers thunder from
the holy mountain.

Psalms 3: 3

Worthy!

Imagine my surprise as I prepared for church and glanced out the window to see ducks sitting in my pool. Calmly paddling along the surface with no worries, for they were shielded on all sides by the pool deck and the foliage. The only place they could expect predators was from above and that was an area they were confident in enough to sit down in my pool. As they paddled around, I thought to be careful not to startle them but I opened the door and my dog walked out to the edge of the pool, he barked and they stayed placid swimming to the opposite side of the pool. The dog decided they weren't bothered by him so he went on about his business and so did they; content in their world which had just collided with mine. I have pondered it especially as they were there again yesterday when I got home, unbothered by our comings and goings. I thought why now after being here for over ten years is this the first time and realized it was Rudy. Rudy was our ferocious and fearless terrier who barked at everyone and everything, loved playing ball but also defended the whole yard from all things wild from snakes to deer. The deer have been eating my rosebuds now in his absence. God, unlike Rudy who has passed on, is a constant shield. He keeps the predators of life at bay often without our awareness of the things He has done. His very presence is our shield. He keeps us grounded and stable in spite of buffeting storms. He lifts our heads high even when we feel low. He is our Father and our source. Are you tired of fighting it all? David says that with all his might, he shouted to God and God's answers thundered from the Holy Mountain. God isn't a patsy or a genie. He is God. He is also our Father. When we cry out in our desperation, He hears our cries and His answer thunders back...I have loved you with an everlasting love...seek me and you will find me. He is worthy no matter what our circumstances because He has been there all along. He isn't leaving us or deserting us because times are tough. He is faithful, true and just. Lean in. Trust the process. He is God. Cry out as David did and hear His answer thunder. Let Him ground you and lift your head in confidence that you are surrounded with His shield on all sides. He will protect you. He will provide and He will guide. As sunset came, the ducks flew to roost for the night. They knew the night was coming and they knew that their shelter awaited. God, please hear our cry. We need you as never before to be our source of peace and provision in these hours of uncertainty around us.
We trust in you for you are worthy of it all.

"He replied to the one speaking for the rest, 'Friend, I haven't been unfair. We agreed on the wage of a dollar, didn't we? So take it and go. I decided to give to the one who came last the same as you. Can't I do what I want with my own money? Are you going to get stingy because I am generous?'

"Here it is again, the Great Reversal: many of the first ending up last, and the last first."

Matthew 20: 13-16

Fair!

The game of life is at play and there are winners and losers, not by luck but by choice. In Matthew, Jesus shared a story of a boss who hired workers throughout a day for labor then ended up paying each of them the same wage whether they had worked for one hour or eight. Naturally, those who labored longer got upset feeling like the wage was unfairly distributed. Jesus used this story as an illustration of the Kingdom of God. Many people get incensed that someone who has done wrong most of their life then repents gets the same response from Christ as the one who spent their entire life in service or in terms of perceived blessings here on Earth, the one who has done wrong is blessed when someone who diligently serves God still struggles in health or wealth. I used to tell my students "life isn't fair, get over it and make the best of your circumstances". Why? Because the truth is that we all have choices and perceptions. We make mistakes. We falsely accuse and reward based on our own perceptions of our reality. There is a saying that one man's junk is another's treasure, meaning that our values differ and what one sees as wealth, another may perceive as waste. The light breaks across the sky in the clouds after the storm and the rainbow of colors are scattered. The same light shone but each cloud reflected the light differently giving an assortment of color and patterns to the eye. Beauty is in the eye of the beholder and fairness is a perception of mankind. Is it fair that God's only son sacrificed His life as an atonement for our sins? Is any of us truly more worthy than another of that sacrifice? The truth is that all of Earth is God's. Some people look at their situation and see themselves as under a curse while another looks at that same person thinking how blessed they are. We are human. We always think others have it better or worse. We always compare ourselves to others no matter what but the reality is that God is not concerned with our perceptions unless they are aligned in His will. Just as Jesus shared with this story, the boss hired certain people and agreed on a wage then hired others for the same wage but fewer hours. Does this seem unfair? Sure it does if we are comparing labor and time but the reality is that the agreed upon wage was paid! Fairness isn't equality. There is no such thing as equality or inequality in God's kingdom truthfully. We are not equal to God, the angels nor to one another. We are all His. We are all uniquely blessed and designed. No, life isn't fair. Ups and downs happen. We win and we lose. We choose well and we choose poorly. The only thing that matters is our stance with God. The only equality that exists is in Him. He states clearly that the wages of sin is death but the gift of God is eternal life. Herein lies the choice. The Great Reversal is that many get caught up in the wrong minded thoughts of fairness in God's kingdom. Blessings come to all of us. Sorrows and challenges do too. We can bemoan our gains and losses or we can celebrate that Christ gave us equal opportunity to choose Him. The true measure of equality or fairness is in, that while we were yet sinners, lost and without hope, Christ made a way to bridge the great divide created by our desire for equality. Lucifer lost out on the Blessed Hope because he chose his desire for equality over his love for God. Each of us has the same choice and chance. Life isn't fair but through Jesus we all have the choice, the opportunity to be redeemed-choose repentance and choose Him. Fair-For All In Repentance.

"But if you just use my words in Bible studies and don't work them into your life, you are like a stupid carpenter who built his house on the sandy beach. When a storm rolled in and the waves came up, it collapsed like a house of cards."

Matthew 7: 26-27

Used!

Have you ever been used up and tossed aside by another person as if you didn't matter? This is a very painful thing to endure. It is the cause of many heartbreaks and ruined lives. Using and not acting upon God's word is an example of this lack of understanding. Misapplication of God's word or just using it to fit our moment and not working it into the patterns of our lives is like this to God. He compares the person who uses the word without truly working it in as an unwise builder who didn't choose a firm foundation to build his house upon. We have had so much rain lately that the ground is saturated and this causes sandy soil to shift and move and easily get carried away in water. Anything put upon a sandy soil quickly gets inundated with water then runoff causes it to get carried away and not anchored. I have seen many "fads" of scripture usage come and go. Usage of God's word for the moment but no solid anchoring. Quoting it but not believing it; sharing it but never knowing it and even people raised in church on it but never understanding it. God's promises are anchors for our souls and we must quit being buoyed about by every storm that comes our way. I admit that some of these storms are doozies of our own making and they knock our feet right out from under us filling us with fear and trepidation but God hasn't given that to us and as we anchor in Him steadfastly, we can have God confidence that He is in control. Unexpected and devastating storms happen. They often change our trajectory of life on this Earth whether those storms be physical, mental, financial or emotional. Our lives when fixed on Him may weather big storms and it may change the current or flow of our lives drastically from where we thought we were headed but He is still the Master of the Wind. He still speaks peace and He still calms situations that seem to be torrential hurricanes in our lives. Choose to anchor and work God's word into life. Begin to build a solid foundation on who He is and not what the circumstances say. The storms will come, the waves will roll in, the shifting sands of life will be washed and moved but if we anchor our hope in who He is and not in what the storm seems to be saying then we can hear His still small voice through the winds and waves saying "Peace, be still" and "Let Go, Let Me Speak to the Storm". This life is a house of cards no matter who we think we are. This life is nothing more than dust and air but He has given us eternity to rest in Him. Working the words of God into the life we build establishes a solid foundation that lasts despite the troubles. Whatever the circumstances, His words can still be worked into our lives to have living power. Speak to the storm that The Master is saying Peace Be Still.

As they were leaving Jericho, a huge crowd followed. Suddenly they came upon two blind men sitting alongside the road. When they heard it was Jesus passing, they cried out, "Master, have mercy on us! Mercy, Son of David!" The crowd tried to hush them up, but they got all the louder, crying, "Master, have mercy on us! Mercy, Son of David!" Jesus stopped and called over, "What do you want from me?"

They said, "Master, we want our eyes opened. We want to see!"

Deeply moved, Jesus touched their eyes. They had their sight back that very instant, and joined the procession.

Matthew 20: 29-34

Sight!

My eyes have been bothering me so I went to the optometrist who told me my vision had improved. He said my brain had trained one eye to see at a distance and another up close so the dominant eye swaps depending on what I am doing and that swap is the uncomfortable moments I have been having. It is amazing how when we are told the reason behind a perceived issue how our perspective changes. As Jesus was walking out of Jericho in huge crowds, two blind beggars heard He was coming and decided they wanted a situational change. They called out begging for His attention but they were almost hushed and ignored by the crowd...instead they realized that a quiet moment wasn't going to achieve sight, so they began to get really loud and they caught His attention. The verse said Jesus was deeply moved and touched their eyes which immediately restored their vision, then they joined the crowd following Him. They didn't take No, Hush, Quiet, or Stop. They pursued their vision. Our vision of the Truth of who He is in our lives gets lost in the noise and crowd of this life. We sit on the sidelines allowing the visions to remain dim when the Master Healer is walking in our presence. He can restore our lives to better than ever before if we, but call out about the noise, despite those telling us to hush...scream out to God, oh God, how I need you to touch my eyes so I might have your vision restored into my life. Don't let the clutter and clamor of life dim the truth of His coming drawing close. Call out. Jesus stopped and asked, "what do you want from me?" They said, "Master, we want our eyes opened. We want to see!" Their deep desire for vision and change of their situation caused them to overcome the noises of life teeming around them. If we want to deeply move the heart of God to hear our cry, then we must ignore those trying to hush us and push through the noisy crowds of life into His presence. Jesus is asking, "What do you want from me?" Master, I want my eyes opened....I want to see you, Jesus! I want to reach out and touch You and tell you how I love You. Pursue His presence, His vision and Him...this is what true sight is. What moves the heart of God deeply time after time in scripture is persistent faith despite the noise of the crowd of circumstances. Open our eyes, Lord. Let us be in your presence with your vision and sight restored in our lives. Hear our cries.

But Jesus was matter-of-fact: "Yes– and if you embrace this kingdom life and don't doubt God, you'll not only do minor feats like I did to the fig tree, but also triumph over huge obstacles. This mountain, for instance, you'll tell, 'Go jump in the lake,' and it will jump. Absolutely everything, ranging from small to large, as you make it a part of your believing prayer, gets included as you lay hold of God."

Matthew 21: 21-22

Triumph!

What has always fascinated me about this portion of scripture is that Jesus has been going around with his disciples for months healing, touching, doing miracles that are just flabbergasting and then he is hungry so he walks up to the fig tree and looks for figs on the tree to eat and there's no fruit so he curses the tree to never have fruit again and the tree withers completely down immediately in front of the disciples eyes to a stick. I'm not shocked that the tree listened to Jesus. I'm shocked that the disciples were so surprised and yet we are so much like them. At least I am. I have seen so many miracles in my life. Wonderful miracles that are beyond belief, things like cancer falling out of people and legs growing in lengths and crazy wonderful unbelievable things happening before my eyes and yet somehow, I still allow doubt to walk with me when I walk through my everyday life as if that is my partner instead of Jesus. I still get weighed down and overwhelmed by the things of this world, such as finances and health and emotional trauma, when I know that the Master has control over all of these things, and I should be at peace. The disciples were blown away that the tree just withered and died before their eyes because Jesus said that it would bear no more fruit. Jesus was very matter-of-fact, because he knew what he said would happen, and he had no doubt. He says in the scripture in Matthew, that if we embrace the kingdom life and don't doubt God that we will not only do minor things such as that which was so major to those disciples and to us but we would also triumph over huge obstacles. He points to a mountain and says to His disciples and to us, You can tell the Mountain to throw itself into the sea and it will do so at your command, if you believe. He says absolutely everything from big to small if you make it a part of your believing life, gets included into your God life, when you lay hold of God. I so desire to walk in His power and strength. I so desire to walk in this place of faith where the things of earth don't weigh so heavily on me, but I am so like the man who struggled with believing so he said Lord, please help me believe. I often get into impossible situations and I have no idea how they are going to work out but I do trust that God will make a way, which He does. Often it doesn't look like I think it will. This is what the disciples saw. They had no doubt that the tree wouldn't produce fruit again when Jesus said so but they were shocked that the tree withered to a stick. Why? Because in our minds, spiritual things don't exist on the same mortal plane as our everyday life. We walk in two frames of mind: the mortal and the spiritual. We must merge the two and begin fully walking in His spirit in order for things of Earth to be subject to things of the Spirit in our lives. We don't command mountains to move because we have mortal equipment to move them. We ask only for the impossible because it is outside our control. The large things we implore, intercede and believe for but Jesus works in the small things too. Nothing big or small is impossible for God. What is it that we are needing in our lives? We need to lay hold of God as never before to see His mighty hand move in our lives.

When I call, give me answers.
God, take my side!
Once, in a tight place, you gave me room;
Now I'm in trouble again: grace me! hear me!

Look at this: look
Who got picked by God!
He listens the split second I call to him.
Complain if you must, but don't lash out.
Keep your mouth shut,
and let your heart do the talking.
Build your case before God
and wait for his verdict.
Why is everyone hungry for more?
"More, more," they say.
"More, more."
I have God's more-than-enough,
More joy in one ordinary day
Than they get in all their shopping sprees.
At day's end I'm ready for sound sleep,
For you, God, have put my life back together.

Psalms 4: 1, 3-8

Picked!

One Sunday in Children's church, I watched as the children picked teams and I saw the anxious faces as they waited on their names to be called. I have often felt this anxiety as did David in this passage where he calls upon God to take his side. He says now I am in trouble again, a tight place then in joy, he hollers look, I got picked by God! Building your case before God isn't hard, we do that well but the waiting place while keeping your mouth shut from complaining about His timing is another thing altogether. More. What are we seeking more of in our daily routines? More peace and joy or more of something to complain about? God is God. He sees us and knows us as no other. The rose in this picture is a sunset rose. The colors are a changing variety as the flower fully opens. It gradually reveals its glory to the world as it continues to unfold. Our life is God's revelation. Pain, anxiety, financial woes, irritations, cancer, health, etc...none is too big or small for God. At the end of this day of life, we will be ready to rest in Him from all of these because He is the source who pulls it all together. Make your case before God: Hear me God, pick me! Grace me with your glory and presence today. Let me be the one chosen to worship you in spirit and truth. Let me be the one who experiences your miracles and feels your touch. Let me be the rose unfolding in your presence to reveal your glory. Pick me! Hear my heart for more of you and less of me. Bless me with joy. Wipe out my stress. Let me be graced with your peace and contentment in confidence of your anointing. Pick me God, for you God are the only one who can put my life back together. Once I was in a tight place and you gave me room to breathe and be at peace so I could open into your presence. Now I am in trouble again! Pick me God! I want to be on your team! I know you win! I know you will give me assurance. Pick me God!

The very credentials these people are waving around as something special, I'm tearing up and throwing out with the trash—along with everything else I used to take credit for. And why? Because of Christ. Yes, all the things I once thought were so important are gone from my life. Compared to the high privilege of knowing Christ Jesus as my Master, firsthand, everything I once thought I had going for me is insignificant—dog dung. I've dumped it all in the trash so that I could embrace Christ and be embraced by him. I didn't want some petty, inferior brand of righteousness that comes from keeping a list of rules when I could get the robust kind that comes from trusting Christ— God's righteousness.

Philippians 3: 7-9

Robust!

Vigorous! Healthy! Prosperous! Booming! Potent! Powerful! These are the synonyms for robust. Paul describes God's righteousness as robust! Active and moving....not staid and stale, not fake or washed up but alive in power! I love this! I am in love with the Northern Lights as pictured here through the lens of an ice-cave. I think they fascinate me because they are a symbol of unconventional, incontestable and uncontrolled power! They symbolize all that God is to me: something we can occasionally see but is always there. But God tells us that His power is alive in us and Paul describes it as robust. Does it mean we don't have trouble in this world? No! Unfortunately, there is a lot of it but Paul who had experienced his share of it for sure said that he counts all the good as loss and is more than happy to suffer for Christ. Why? To live is for Christ and in Christ but to die we gain as we go to Christ. Having troubles is a part of living. But how we approach those troubles is how we are determined to be His or naught. I have had my share of problems and many are of my own making through less than brilliant decisions but Christianity isn't about perfection, it is about resurrection. Mistakes lead us to the cross where His blood poured out and from there we can lay it all down at His feet and move forward in redemption. When asked by a very intelligent young lawyer what was the most important thing in life, Jesus answered that we love God with all we have. If we love things, dreams and people more than God, then we miss the first and most important commandment which is to love God with ALL we are and ever will be. It is this supreme love that activates the faith that moves the mountains in our lives. We cannot simply trudge on day by day striving to find happiness in our earthly portal because it isn't attainable except through Him. He created us with a God sized hole and nothing will fill it except Him and when we are not constantly filled with Him, we are open to discontent. Discontentment is one of the worst things a person can experience because it is perpetual unhappiness that consumes all a person is and does. God doesn't exist in this place but He is near to call upon. Picture this. You are sitting in this ice house freezing and unhappy but just outside is the warm light of God's love. You must step out into His forgiving arms to experience it though. You can see it from your window but to feel it embrace you, you must step into it. I think the wonder of these lights in person is likely a completely overwhelming experience of spiritual magnitude but no greater than the warm embrace available daily just by calling on His name. Sometimes our blessings come through trials and hard times because that is how we appreciate the miracle the most. People who have never experienced pain aren't as grateful to walk around in no pain. People who have never experienced loss do not understand the value of love relationships like those who have. People who have never struggled financially or emotionally or spiritually do not understand the same level of appreciation felt by those who have felt that wonder of His redeeming power. Take all those things that matter so much and leave them at the cross. It is through the breaking of the light via magnetic forces that comes the wonder of the northern lights. Think of the wonderful light you bring to the kingdom through this breaking moment. Breathe. If our blessings come through tears, it is worth the moments. When the challenges come, step out of the ice house into His wonderful lights of love. No matter what, He is still God.

For whoever desires to save his life will lose it, but whoever loses his life for My sake and the gospel's will save it. For what will it profit a man if he gains the whole world, and loses his own soul? Or what will a man give in exchange for his soul?

Mark 8: 35-37

Profit!

Gain, ambition, drive, getting ahead in the race of life is what we are taught from birth by the actions of those around us. Push harder, stronger, go tougher, try more...but Jesus says what will it profit a man if he gains the whole world at his feet but loses his soul. Ambition isn't the enemy and neither is profit but if it takes the seat of God's presence in our lives, it steals our true purpose then we become lost. What will we be willing to sacrifice for our own souls? Jesus was willing to give His life for our souls and He did. But what are we willing to give up? Our dreams, our plans, our hopes...our wealth, health and intellect are all value systems that we invest in heavily. What are we willing to do for Jesus? A flower lives for the purpose of producing seed and growth for the plant. We look at the flower or the fruit as the ultimate result but in truth, that flower or fruit is only the bearer of the future growth of that plant. The life of the plant is in the root. The resulting beauty and fragrance of the flower is to draw the bees to the nectar so that the flower sustains the life of the plant into the future. We are to be about the Father's business of drawing life to Him and reproducing that which will draw others to Him so that they too will carry the life forward. We get caught up in our situations and desires and futures and wants, striving to gain it all. At what cost? Is that one thing we desire worth our soul? Not too long ago, I experienced a setback in my life because of choices I made which resulted in hurting many people around me unintentionally. I didn't keep my eyes on the Lord but rather moved my view to my temporal future. In eagerness to move forward, I made choices that I regret. Now those choices didn't kill me nor did they ruin my life forever but they did hurt myself and others. My hopes and dreams put ahead of God's timing got out of alignment causing a wreck in my life. What does it profit a person to gain all but lose their soul? What is the thing, dream, hope, etc. that you are putting ahead of God in your life? What are you willing to lay down for Him? If you keep putting yourself first, you are set on a collision course because you are not in alignment with Him. Alignment is important because it keeps us on the right track. Focusing on Him allows us to experience His fullness, grace and mercies, new every morning and our dreams become reality in His timing. Whoever desires to save his own lifestyle and ways will lose his soul but whoever will be willing to sacrifice it all for God's ways, will gain eternity. This doesn't mean we cannot have our hopes, dreams, wishes and plans but it does mean we must leave it in His hands to make it come about as it should. Lay it down. Yield it and watch the beauty He can make from the shattered dreams. Stained glass takes broken pieces.

"Don't let people do that to you, put you on a pedestal like that. You all have a single Teacher, and you are all classmates. Don't set people up as experts over your life, letting them tell you what to do. Save that authority for God; let him tell you what to do. No one else should carry the title of 'Father'; you have only one Father, and he's in heaven. And don't let people maneuver you into taking charge of them. There is only one Life-Leader for you and them—Christ.

"Do you want to stand out? Then step down. Be a servant. If you puff yourself up, you'll get the wind knocked out of you. But if you're content to simply be yourself, your life will count for plenty.

Matthew 23: 8-12

Titles!

We all wear a lot of hats or titles in our lives that are roles we play to others. Sometimes we are even unaware of the title or role as we go about our day to day but in other times, we are honored or acknowledged. I have lots of both experiences and my heart thrills when one of my family or friends is honored as my daughter-in-law recently was. Being chosen and honored is a blessing that God gives us without fanfare and without our acknowledgment, He is the expert on our lives. Most of us recognize when someone is an expert and we go to them when we have struggles or concerns in that area for help. We reach out to those who can bridge the gap for us but most of us fail to realize that our Father God has always held the role of Father from creation of time. I have always been an independent individual to a certain extent but I love to be loved and cherished. My feeling of honoring isn't a lot of accolades but rather genuine truth spoken and acknowledging my efforts. I think God is so much more than we realize in that He not only sees all, and is all, but He desires acknowledgment from us that He is our all. Sometimes I struggle with balancing all the hats or roles that I have, that I feel like in all the juggling, I fail to accomplish all I desire. This disappointment in myself is human nature that we shift over to blame so easily because we do not like the feeling of failure. Failure to accomplish is a way of learning. It is much more painful than success and ease but learning happens through trials and struggles as much or more than times of ease because when we cannot, we turn to Him as we know He can. Jesus instructs us in Matthew to not let people put us up on a pedestal as a leader of spiritual means because we get puffed up and then fall carrying others down with us. He says save the authority of expertise for God, allowing Him to tell you what to do. We have only one Father and He is in Heaven. No one else can carry that title for it is much too heavy and as our Life-leader we can trust that if Jesus Himself submitted His life into His hands, we can too. If we want to stand out then we must first step down and realize His place and authority in our lives. Just be ourselves and let God be the Master of the Wind in our lives.Let Him push our boat of life with His wind and blow us in the directions He desires. Too many times we push and push to be more than He desires and we end up flat on our faces. God is and always will be. Simple trust is all it takes. Choose contentment in whatever He is doing and He will work all things out for our good!

"You're hopeless! What arrogant stupidity! You say, 'If someone makes a promise with his fingers crossed, that's nothing; but if he swears with his hand on the Bible, that's serious.' What ignorance! Does the leather on the Bible carry more weight than the skin on your hands? And what about this piece of trivia: 'If you shake hands on a promise, that's nothing; but if you raise your hand that God is your witness, that's serious'? What ridiculous hairsplitting! What difference does it make whether you shake hands or raise hands? A promise is a promise. What difference does it make if you make your promise inside or outside a house of worship? A promise is a promise. God is present, watching and holding you to account regardless.

Matthew 23: 16-22

Promises!

God is present! Read that again. God says a promise is a promise and He is present, watching and holding us to account. Jesus is so frustrated with the religious leaders for their constantly changing rules and rhetoric. He puts it simply which should refresh us. A promise is a promise whether made in the church or in the day to day. If God said it, He will honor it. His word is full of active promises that He honors in our day to day lives. We are His people. God doesn't split hairs with His words. He isn't out to trick or stub us with His promises. He is true. People often get confused by the why and the wait. Why does God let bad things happen to good people and when is God going to come through on His promises? These are the two top questions that cause people to doubt His promises and lose faith in His providence. I can tell you a story or two of waiting when things were down to the wire but God showed up. I can tell you a story or two of when bad things happened to good people that God allowed for a greater purpose. We get bogged down and lose our peace because of the why/wait. When it seems like God isn't doing what we need in the time we want it, we easily turn on our promises to be faithful to Him and trust Him.

We look at our situation of impossibility and get so turned upside down and frustrated that we give up on the God of the impossible because we doubt His purpose aligning with ours. Scripture tells us that men and women are fickle promise keepers but God always keeps His word. The timing is the doubt starter. God's timing isn't always ours and His ways are not always ours. We have such a need to have it in our timing and our way that we are used to forcing it when God is busy at work. Time after time in scripture we see that God was at work behind the scenes but I am sure as Daniel was lowered into the lions' den, his heart was pounding in fear...and I know Esther quaked as she went before the king because scripture says so. David was prolific in his songs of doubt and fear as well as praise and glory. Abraham had a child with his maid because he got tired of waiting too. Waiting is a human foible. We struggle with patience and waiting. We don't understand why our situation isn't moving the hand of God urgently. We get tired in the waiting but then we are reminded that His promises are true. Let me encourage you and encourage myself in the Lord. The waiting is only the period of refining for the promise. Joseph became a great leader because the trials he went through taught him to appreciate the struggle. Paul went from a life of leisure to a life on the run for God because he knew God was real. Hold onto His promises. The ride may get rocky but stay in the boat with Him despite it all because he truly cares for us and His promises are true no matter what it looks like to us. Keep your promise you made to God to give Him your whole life and lean in for surely He will provide.

"Staying with it—that's what God requires. Stay with it to the end. You won't be sorry, and you'll be saved. All during this time, the good news—the Message of the kingdom—will be preached all over the world, a witness staked out in every country. And then the end will come.

"Take a lesson from the fig tree. From the moment you notice its buds form, the merest hint of green, you know summer's just around the corner. So it is with you: When you see all these things, you'll know he's at the door. Don't take this lightly. I'm not just saying this for some future generation, but for all of you. This age continues until all these things take place. Sky and earth will wear out; my words won't wear out.

Matthew 24: 13-14, 32-35

Worn!

I am worn out from the struggles this last week, month, year...last ten...I am tired. Sometimes, it feels like giving up is the right path when things get hard. Jesus instructs us in Matthew that things in this world will be hard but He says stay with it. Stay with it to the end and you won't be sorry, you'll be saved. The struggle is real. We are in a battle for eternity, not just here and now. He tells us to take a lesson from the fig tree. Note that as soon as you see signs of the times, prepare, for He is coming again. We hear of people talking about global warming and doomsday videos of Earth ending because we know in our hearts, what God has said is true. The Earth and sky will wear out but His words never will. Are you tired? Worn? Heavy? Take it to Jesus. He says His words are always there just as His promises are true. His truth is not that He will do it but that He has already done it. Stay with it. The track may not look finished but He has already made the path for you. I think of water as it flows...going towards this fall and never knowing but the fall is beautiful to me. To the water, it changes the dynamic of the flow as the sudden spill makes a cataclysmic sound and motion. Take a lesson from this waterfall, God isn't finished with you yet. We may have falls that are unexpectedly overwhelming and take our breaths away. It may change the dynamics of everything we know or have known. We may lose everything that has been constant in our surroundings and our lives but He is still God. The landscape around the water influences the water but the water doesn't become another element because of the landscape. The water changes forms from liquid to gas in cataclysmic situations. It changes in freezing weather to a solid and in hot to steam but it is still what God created it to be... teeming with life...the very elements of our breath flow through water. Water is essential to our lives and His living waters are essential to our spirits. Stay with it. No matter what it looks like. Hold on to the end even if it ends up in a waterfall, for He has us. Even if things change drastically for us, He has a course of calm cool rest coming. I think I will take a lesson from the fig tree. Spring is here but summer is on its way. Trials are here but answers are on the way. Circumstances look rough but Jesus is coming soon. All we have to do is press in to Him. He said don't take this lightly, this age only continues until all He has in place happens. He is coming soon. The Message has been preached all over the world now, there are witnesses in every country. This is our sign that the end is drawing near. Take heart; hold on for the ride. His word is drawing us to the edge and over into Glory.

"The Arrival of the Son of Man will take place in times like Noah's. Before the great flood everyone was carrying on as usual, having a good time right up to the day Noah boarded the ark. They knew nothing–until the flood hit and swept everything away. "The Son of Man's Arrival will be like that: Two men will be working in the field–one will be taken, one left behind; two women will be grinding at the mill–one will be taken, one left behind. So stay awake, alert. You have no idea what day your Master will show up. But you do know this: You know that if the homeowner had known what time of night the burglar would arrive, he would have been there with his dogs to prevent the break-in. Be vigilant just like that. You have no idea when the Son of Man is going to show up.

Matthew 24: 39-44

Anticipation!

Anticipation can cause anxiety or excitement. It is a concept of waiting while knowing that something is about to happen but being unable to control the timing of the event. One can anticipate things that they're going through and know the date/time also but the butterfly in the stomach kind of anticipation is weathering the unknown or unexpected. Noah had followed God's instructions to the letter, building the ark, getting the family and animals inside all the while he was preaching to others about the anticipation of an event he was convinced was coming. Noah knew in his heart what God had told him but years of struggle and being made fun of happened. His salvation was also his undoing as far as earthly gain. He lost everything and everyone he knew to build the ark. He was mocked and ridiculed constantly but God had a plan. I cannot imagine a more horrifying experience honestly because I love wide and deep. As I look around me seeing prophecy being fulfilled, I struggle with why people won't hear. We have a world full of self-help and an ugliness towards God that is pervasive. Recently when my first audiobook devotional launched, I was astounded by the complete disregard for God by so many. This society is like an out of control car careening towards the edge of a cliff while the people inside laugh and party without a thought for what is just around the corner. Matthew 24 likens our time/society to that of Noah's. Only where a flood happens in Noah's time, in ours, Jesus will return to catch His bride away. I remember the anticipation of my wedding very well. Lots of planning and preparation had gone into it and the day was swiftly approaching. Excitement flooded the air as everyone prepared for the celebration. Plans were made and travel booked but the unexpected happened. The town lost water that night and no one could shower or bathe. Our wedding was at 10am on a Saturday so no shower on Friday night provided for fragrant guests as they doused themselves in extra perfume and cologne. It didn't matter. The only thing that was on our minds was uniting. We didn't care about anything else...no dampers at all...it was a perfect Cinderella like moment because the long anticipated day had arrived. Jesus is coming and His bride needs to be about His business preparing for His coming. All that needs to be made ready for the wedding supper is in place. At any moment, He will announce His readiness and we will be caught up with Him forever-raptured. I look at the background of this photo-the beautiful northern lights captured in one spectacular moment. That one spectacular moment of His arrival will be final just as the closing of the door on the Ark. Are we ready? Are our eyes on Him and His soon return? Be vigilant because it can happen at any moment!

**Keep vigilant watch over your heart;
that's where life starts.
Don't talk out of both sides
of your mouth;
avoid careless banter, white lies,
and gossip.
Keep your eyes straight ahead;
ignore all sideshow distractions.
Watch your step,
and the road will stretch out
smooth before you.
Look neither right nor left;
leave evil in the dust.**

Proverbs 4: 23-27

Vigilant!

What is our most valuable treasure? God through the wise words of Solomon says it is our hearts. He says that is where life starts. He gives us directions for keeping a vigilant watch on our hearts. Vigilance means that we are not careless nor flippant with our words nor our actions. I can say I have been very hurt by careless words and actions before and even by gossip, white lies, banter and doublespeak. Keeping our eyes on the eternal is very hard when there are so many distractions around drawing us away from where He would lead us. Many times in life, it is hard to see the road ahead. Things look very bleak and discouraging but I know our God and He has a plan and a purpose for us. He knows our comings and goings. His advice to us is to guard our hearts. Our hearts are the place where hope lives and burns. Our hearts are where we cherish our Savior and His promises. Our hearts are where truth reigns and keeps us on track. Guarding our hearts is a wise instruction because out of the abundance of our heart, our mouths speak. If we are full of God then our words are His and led by Him. Careless words hurt me badly this past week. They caused a lot of pain and conflicted immeasurable scars upon my heart because I had not carefully guarded my heart as instructed and I allowed the words to score. The Bible tells us no weapon can come against us and prosper if we are properly armed with His word and are guarding the seat of life. Too many emotional battles have been lost to careless words and deeds by others. Saying things in double-speak or banter isn't meant to harm but does. Writing letters with carelessness (i.e.) about another business or service can be unintentionally painful and hurtful as I have experienced. God says guard our hearts vigilantly not allowing these attacks to become a distraction to our purpose. Remember where our hope is and our purpose is. Keep our eyes straight ahead and not on these sideshows. People are fickle. They will come and go but God who is the anchor of our soul will hold us fast in times of trouble and we must keep our eyes on Him to leave evil in the dust. Leaving evil behind means we must choose not to muddy the waters from a place of pain or hurt. We must be willing to step up and be the difference rather than fight a battle of distraction where our heart is unguarded because we are busy looking in another direction. When things go bad, God is still good...don't fall for Satan's distraction because he is aiming for your heart. If he can get you busy blaming God and looking at how "good" others have it, then he has a shot at your heart treasures of joy, peace, hope, salvation, etc. Scripture tells us that he is out to destroy, steal, kill and maim but Greater is He... the God of all creation than this pedantic little demigod wannabe. What is a vigilant watch over our hearts? Watch our steps (they are ordered of God). Guard our hearts (where He resides). Stay on the path and God will stretch the road out smooth before us. Watch our tongue. Don't speak death; but speak life. Don't speak despair or lack of faith but quote His words of life over our situations. He is greater than any storms. He has good things for us. Just be the You God intended you to be with all that is in you.

"Then the King will say to those on his right, 'Enter, you who are blessed by my Father! Take what's coming to you in this kingdom. It's been ready for you since the world's foundation. And here's why: I was hungry and you fed me, I was thirsty and you gave me a drink, I was homeless and you gave me a room, I was shivering and you gave me clothes, I was sick and you stopped to visit, I was in prison and you came to me.'

Matthew 25: 34-36

Enter!

We stood in line for a long while to get inside the venue. It was beautiful and tranquil, completely fragrant with each and every detail perfect. The peace that came at just knowing all we had worked for had come to fruition meant a lot. Now we could just relax and know that it was all meant to be. The door opened and the King Himself stood there greeting each of us saying "Enter, you who are blessed by my Father! Take what is coming to you in this kingdom. It has been ready for you since the world's foundation."

The dream receded and I am back in bed. My thoughts are still on that moment of peace and tranquility that overcame all the struggles. My mind was captured by His words: You who are blessed by my Father. As we struggle through the days, we long for someone to wrap us in their strong arms and say it's going to be fine. Enter and rest. I know I do. Some days are filled with struggle and worry and failures and fears and heartaches and on and on where the weights just beset us so badly that we falter in our walk. We don't know up from down and just keep plodding to no purpose but to get to the end of our day. Why? Because we forget. We forget that He has said You who are blessed by my Father. We forget His blessings in the midst of our struggles. This world is filled with hardships and overwhelming things but He says that He has overcome all of it. We are His people, his blessed people! We are His. We need to remember this and get our heads out of the impossibilities into the possibles. God Himself, the King of all Glory has called us His blessed because we are His and He charges us with a task to use these blessings to minister to others. What are these ministries? We are to feed the hungry, clothe the cold, visit the sick and those in prison. We are to give Living Water to those who thirst. We are called to be His hand extended and then He can flow through us to others. We take too much upon ourselves so often that we fail to see the WHO He is! He is the King of Glory. He is mighty in battle and strong against all enemies and yet He is humble and soft hearted. He loves those who have given up on themselves as much as He loves any other. He is jealous of us and loves us with an everlasting love. It is time we get our eyes off our circumstances and get our eyes on this King of Glory. He is our answer despite what the circumstances dictate. He is our source, our provision and our love. How eager am I to step back into that place of tranquility and rest but the thing is that I can just by letting Him master it all. As long as I continue to struggle against His call, the dreams cannot be reality. But when I lean into Him and trust with all that is in me, He will be enough. He has always been and will always be from the foundations of the world and He said in His word, that His kingdom has been ready for us since the very foundation of the world. It is ours to walk in. Think about His love, His goodness, His grace and His mercy. Dwell in the House of the Lord today rather than the tents of the wicked. Let our minds be focused on You Lord.

Then Jesus went with them to a garden called Gethsemane and told his disciples, "Stay here while I go over there and pray." Taking along Peter and the two sons of Zebedee, he plunged into an agonizing sorrow. Then he said, "This sorrow is crushing my life out. Stay here and keep vigil with me."

Going a little ahead, he fell on his face, praying, "My Father, if there is any way, get me out of this. But please, not what I want. You, what do you want?"

Matthew 26: 36-39

Vigil!

Sorrow can be a crushing emotion. It can literally wipe out all else leaving you hopeless and feeling meaningless. It is an overwhelming emotion that Jesus experienced at the betrayal of one He loved who walked close to Him. When He was feeling so low, He asked His disciples who were closest to Him to lift Him up in prayer as He was struggling under the weight of that load. They let him down too as their own comfort and ease became more important than their love and concern for Him so they slept. They had no concept of the battle He was waging there in the Garden at Gethsemane. It was the same battle waged and lost in the first Garden of Eden-the battle of flesh/self. The battle was so fierce that Jesus cried drops of blood and sweated blood. His heart was literally broken by the selfishness of humanity and yet He still willingly chose to lay it down. My heart has been broken and I have felt betrayed which is a very crushing experience. It is extremely hard to lift your head and move about under that kind of weight. I also have been the person who failed. The one who caused hurt in another unintentionally but still the pain is felt. What is the root of betrayal? Selfishness. It is the desire for self over others or more specifically my gain at your cost. We see this in life a lot unfortunately as our society has encouraged an "All about me" mindset. We are born into it, raised in it and steeped in it until it is our nature which is why we must lay it all down in order to truly walk where He wants us to walk-in victory. Victory doesn't come without sacrifice. That is the hard part. Just because you have been wronged doesn't give you the victory. Winning isn't the way either. It is only through true repentance which is a turning away from our natural instincts towards the God led choice, even by way of sacrifice, that we achieve His authority in our lives. Many Christians have fallen and failed in this including me. We get so caught up in the selfish desires that it supplants the view of His calling and path. Our way becomes clouded by the seemingly impossible situations then we cry out for salvation. Jesus cried out to God, "My Father, if there is any way, get me out of this. But please not what I want, but what You want." He could have called ten thousand angels and they would've come but He won the battle of Calvary there in that Garden of Prayer when He laid down His will for that of the Father. It isn't easy. It is a soul deep, heart wrenching, physical, mental, emotional and spiritual battle. It can only be conquered in a mindset of continuous prayer. From that moment, Jesus walked in His Father's will. He laid His life down in that moment when He surrendered it all. Surrender is Giving up all of you to become all He desires. He says, "Take up your cross and follow me and I will make you fishers of men". What do you need to surrender? What have you placed on the altar of self which has taken precedence over Him? Nothing and no one can stand before Him uncleanly filled with selfish ambition. He desires what is best for us but He requires we be willing to lay it all at His feet. What is your vigil? What is the thing worth staying awake in time of sleeping? Is He worthy of your vigil? Your sacrifice?

Lord, I surrender all I am to you. Do with me what you will no matter what it costs. Easy to say, Hard to do.

Jesus said, "Put your sword back where it belongs. All who use swords are destroyed by swords. Don't you realize that I am able right now to call to my Father, and twelve companies—more, if I want them—of fighting angels would be here, battle-ready? But if I did that, how would the Scriptures come true that say this is the way it has to be?"

Matthew 26: 52-54

Able!

Able means having the ability to do what one desires to do but it does not offset choice. While working with some students, I understand that their mindset has been in survival mode so long (fight/flight) that they must be treated with velvet gloves. They must have firm direction to give them boundaries but it must be delivered in love and expectation of them making good choices. As Jesus was accosted in the Garden, the disciples had awoken suddenly from their slumber and they went immediately into fight or flight survival mode. One fought by pulling his sword, the others scattered and ran. Jesus had prayed through His battle and knew the rest that was to come. At that moment of yielding, He had a choice. He had already fought and won this battle in prayer so the fight/flight was yielded in Him to the will of The Father. Why is this important for us to grasp? Because we have a natural tendency to "shoot first and ask questions later". We flare up and respond when sometimes it would be most appropriate to stay calm and use good judgment which allows God to fight our battles. When people do us wrong, God is still greater. We may not see the immediate results but we can be confident knowing that He will set all things right. The disciple who swung the sword was reacting in anger because he had fallen asleep during the real battle. His eyes got heavy and he missed the yielding so his immediate reaction was fight. Then Jesus calmly healed the offended person and instructed All that He could have called thousands of angels to His rescue, but He was yielding willingly to a higher purpose. This is incredibly hard to do and has to be done over and over again for while Jesus was God, He was also man and we know He experienced Godly anger which by example of most of the Old Testament is stout! We see in scripture of Him running people out of the temple and turning over tables in frustration. We can be angry and not sin but it is the choice that matters. How our story would be different if Jesus hadn't yielded over and over again to the humiliation of man against God. In silence He suffers as His heart breaks for those who profess to know Him and yet angrily accost Him. As my first devotional book went into audio recording sales, I was shocked at the nasty messages I got as comments on the promotion. Many people do not know God intimately and deeply which has turned them vile and dismissive of the One who gave all for them. Jesus says to us, put back your sword where it belongs because all who use the sword are destroyed by them, meaning let God fight your battles. He isn't saying not to take care or defend yourselves from hurt or malice. He isn't saying to not protect ourselves in wisdom. He is saying for us not to take the path of striking out in anger, for that path is not God's way. The same Jesus who healed blinded eyes could easily have struck all of them blind and escaped but He chose to follow the path of righteousness and yielded His desires to not suffer to the will of The Father. In our lives, we often have troubles and our nature demands we strike back but God is saying to let Him fight our battles. Trust Him to make all things right. I don't claim to understand it all and I have experienced my own share of hurt, devastation and betrayal but I do believe in Him that is greater. Lord, I lay down my carnal weapons of warfare at your feet and pick up my Holy weapons of your word, faith, salvation and truth. I claim your promises upon my situations and ask that you move mightily into these battles taking over all and showing what only God can do.

The Life-Light was the real thing:
Every person entering Life
he brings into Light.
He was in the world,
the world was there through him,
and yet the world didn't even notice.
He came to his own people,
but they didn't want him.
But whoever did want him,
who believed he was who he claimed
and would do what he said,
He made to be their true selves,
their child-of-God selves.
These are the God-begotten,
not blood-begotten,
not flesh-begotten,
not sex-begotten.

John 1: 9-13

Reality!

The real reason we live and breathe and move gets lost in our day to day struggle. Things get hard and we cannot see the light from the bottom of the pit we are stuck in. Perhaps that pit is health or finance or emotional turmoil or just all of it in one ball. Getting our mind from one point to the next can be super challenging and when you are focusing on the muck, it is all you can see. John walked with Jesus and he testified that The Life-Light or Jesus was the real thing. Entering into His Light out of the darkness of our own personal suffering is challenging because it is like walking into a different reality. He created this world and all that is in it. He has control over all and yet many times it seems that our world is careening out of control without any divine intervention at all. His word says "whoever did want Him, who believed He was who He claimed He was and would do what He said He would do, He made them to be their true selves-the child of God selves". God begotten. That is the reality but oh how the tough times look like the real world is all about the here and now. There are days that we just breathe through minute by minute unsure if we are going to make it then there are days of laughter, joy and celebration. Each of us is Born of the flesh with DNA of man/woman (that was created by God) but we by choice, can choose to be the Begotten of God. He made us. We are His. We just forget whose we are. We get caught up in all that tangles us up in this world and we begin to get off balance spinning out of control until we finally yield it all to Him or choose to continue the ultimate demise. It isn't easy. I don't imagine any of the folks in scripture would say it was, as I cannot find one who had it all easy-even King Solomon who was blessed with wisdom and wealth had burdens. What I do see is that God was there through the struggles and made it all possible even when it looked like He had forgotten who they were...Joseph languished in prison, Daniel got thrown into a den of lions, Ruth lost everything including her husband and was begging in a field, etc. In every situation, even those of our own foolish creation, He is still God and He is still able. I don't know what every burden is like because I haven't carried them all but I have my fair share, I promise you that. I don't know how. I don't know when. I am often discouraged and beset by worries too. But no matter what, I do believe He is who He said He was and He will do what He says He will do. It may not look like you want it to but He will still be there right in the nick of time. He created all there is and all there is, is subject to Him. I believe you God. No matter what it looks like. No matter what doctors say or people say or circumstances look like, I choose to believe.

Hurry with your answer, God!
I'm nearly at the end of my rope.
Don't turn away; don't ignore me!
That would be certain death.
If you wake me each morning with the
sound of your loving voice,
I'll go to sleep each night trusting
in you.
Point out the road I must travel;
I'm all ears, all eyes before you.
Save me from my enemies, God—
you're my only hope!
Teach me how to live to please you,
because you're my God.
Lead me by your blessed Spirit
into cleared and level pastureland.

Psalms 143: 7-10

Knotted!

My dog was whining and woke me up. He had been having trouble and been trying to resolve it himself for a while. He couldn't see what the problem was, only that his bed, that was his happy place, was now going with him everywhere he went and he was stuck. He had whined for a while but I ignored it because I couldn't understand why he was whining, I mean he was in his bed, warm and snug...but he was stuck. His comfort had become his trap. His collar had caught onto the fabric and so everywhere he moved, his bed went with him. I finally figured it out and reached down to help him but he kept running away pulling his bed with him instead of being still. Finally, when he quieted and allowed me, I was able to release him. We are so like this! At least I am. We get spun up and stuck in our own messes and then we are so stirred up that we keep making our situations worse until they hit the place of the impossible. Even then, we often push more instead of just being still and trusting God. We are like David in this passage of psalms. Hurry Up God! We made this mess and we are stuck without the ability to resolve it. When answers don't come immediately, we feel like God is ignoring us. When we get our eyes off of these things and onto Him, there is a peace. But doing that is hard. So you start with baby steps. First, stop fighting and worrying and fretting. None of these do anything except cause more issues and anxiety. Next we call on God. Whining if we must, crying, hollering, whatever it takes to let Him know we are desperate for Him. Then begin to count our blessings...one by one... starting with the fact we woke up to the morning even if it feels like that's not a blessing with problems looming ahead...count and settle your mind on Him. God, we need your direction. Point out the roads we must travel. We are listening and looking for you to deliver us from our impossible situations with your supreme ability that is beyond what we can ask or think. Save us God, we call out like David did. You are our only hope. Teach us how to live to please you alone...because you are our God. Lead us by your blessed Spirit into a place of rest and safety where we can be content in you. Getting out of impossible places isn't easy and like a wet knot, it might have to be cut. But if we will be still, hear His voice and trust Him in complete faith. He will deliver.

Who can find a virtuous wife?
For her worth is far above rubies.
The heart of her husband safely trusts her;
So he will have no lack of gain.
She does him good and not evil
All the days of her life.

Strength and honor are her clothing;
She shall rejoice in time to come.
She opens her mouth with wisdom,
And on her tongue is the law of kindness.

Charm is deceitful and beauty is passing,
But a woman who fears the Lord, she shall be
praised. Give her of the fruit of her hands,
And let her own works praise her in the gates.

Proverbs 31: 10-12, 25-26, 30-31

Precious!

The Proverbs 31 woman describes the value of a wife that is in Solomon's wisdom, given by God beyond compare. I read this again this morning and I cried because often I feel like I am a failure and cannot measure up but God says that a woman who fears God SHALL be praised. Shall is a stronger word than Will because it indicates not only a future but a promise. God's promises are without fail and His mercies are beyond compare. Solomon had all the world could offer. He had riches, beautiful people surrounding him, and wisdom from God but he asked "Who can find a virtuous wife?" as if he understood the value of such without possessing this. I honestly don't know if he had a great wife or two as in those days it was the custom to have multiple wives. What I do know is that I have given all I have to God to use and turn into good for Him. I know I have given of every means I have in faithfully serving Him and He has been faithful to me. Right now, things are not perfect and life has difficulties in lots of places but I am so blessed. I am blessed to be called wife, mother, daughter, boss, friend, colleague, etc. but most of all Child of God. It says here, "Give her of the fruit of her hands; And let her own works praise her in the gates". This morning as I think about my momma and all the mommas I know who have given their all, I am reminded that when we give it all to Jesus, He says He will take all our sorrows and turn them into joy. What is it that you are holding onto? Give it all to Him and He will make it worth far more than rubies. Ruby is my birthstone so this has special meaning to me. Our worth isn't determined by our strength and honor-those are our clothes. Our worth isn't determined by our wealth or abilities nor even our successes which receive accolades. Our worth is found in our virtue towards God. A woman who fears and respects God Will receive all He has promised because He is the Great I Am. When you get tired of chasing the pretty rainbows and spinning round, turn it all over and He can take all the sorrows and turn them into Joys!

From noon to three, the whole earth was dark. Around mid-afternoon Jesus groaned out of the depths, crying loudly, "Eli, Eli, lama sabachthani?" which means, "My God, my God, why have you abandoned me?"

At that moment, the Temple curtain was ripped in two, top to bottom. There was an earthquake, and rocks were split in pieces. What's more, tombs were opened up, and many bodies of believers asleep in their graves were raised. (After Jesus' resurrection, they left the tombs, entered the holy city, and appeared to many.)

Matthew 27: 45-46, 51-53

Abandoned!

Are you feeling bereft and abandoned? Like riding a roller coaster of emotions, our faith has to hold us in times of extreme emotional stress because it is then when we are weak in body and spirit and mind from constant attack that Satan tries his wiles. Jesus had been betrayed, beaten and crucified. He was emotionally, physically and mentally spent and at that moment, He called out to God, "Father, why have you abandoned me?" We know from scripture that was the final moment of yielding-extreme faith. When Jesus gave it all despite feeling abandoned, He said, "Father, into Your hands, I commit my Spirit." Wow! Grasp this. The Godhead 3 in 1 seen in this one moment and one phrase. The moment Jesus yielded, miraculously people were raised from the dead, an earthquake occurred that opened the graves and split the temple veil which kept us separated from God. Now the bridge across the divide between God and man was completely made. The bridge was the cross. The building of it was the crucifixion but the power of it remains in the yielding. I don't know about you but I do not like getting in over my head in anything as that lack of certainty causes me anxieties. Faith walking requires uncertainty in circumstances but certainty in Him who is able. God says in His word that He would never leave us but that doesn't mean that emotionally we don't feel abandoned. It means that when we feel abandoned, we are in the faith walk-walking into the flames like the 3 Hebrews, walking into the lions' den like Daniel, into the king's throne room like Esther, into the unknown like Ruth, into the sea then the belly of the whale like Jonah, into extreme loss like Job, into prison like Joseph, Paul, Silas, Barnabas....and so many others, into boiling oil like John, and the list goes on. Our abandoned feelings are the beginning of the true faith walk where we do not understand why, how, when or even if but we do hold onto the promise that He is faithful no matter what the circumstances dictate. He cannot be less than who He is. He is God. He is the same God who raised Lazarus and healed blinded eyes. He is the same yesterday, today and forever. Emotions are high during hard trials but if we ride the waves of His love, He will sustain us. We just need to find our footing in Him to walk on those waters and command the storms. Lord, let us have the faith to be a wave walker in the direst of circumstances. Let us keep our eyes on you even when we cannot see you.

How can a young person live a clean life?
By carefully reading the map of your Word.
I'm single-minded in pursuit of you;
don't let me miss the road signs you've posted.
I've banked your promises in the vault of my
heart so I won't sin myself bankrupt.
Be blessed, God;
train me in your ways of wise living.
I'll transfer to my lips
all the counsel that comes from your mouth;
I delight far more in what you tell me about
living than in gathering a pile of riches.
I ponder every morsel of wisdom from you,
I attentively watch how you've done it.
I relish everything you've told me of life,
I won't forget a word of it.

Psalms 119: 9-16

Bankrupt!

The difference in bankruptcy and banked savings is the saving itself-the investing into a sure thing. In Psalms, David instructs young people that a clean life starts with a single-minded pursuit of God. He asks God to direct him with signs and to help him not to miss the signs while being distracted by all that life offers. We know from looking at David's life that he was far from perfect and he did miss the road sometimes getting off track. God called him a man after his heart for one reason alone, the banked promises of God which David pursued. He delighted in God more than money or any other thing. We cannot think his life was easy. In fact, as far as financial things, he was often without early in his life especially while he lived on the run from Saul despite being anointed of God. Anointing doesn't promise perfection in life nor a problem free life. In fact, pursuing God often brings the attention of Satan himself in attacks against us in so many ways that if we haven't banked His word into our hearts, it can be hard to see up from the depths. David requests God to train him in the ways of wise living so he can transfer to his own lips the wise counsel that comes from God and he says he banks God's promises into the vault of his heart so he will not sin himself bankrupt. Pondering on Godly wisdom, counsel and His promises is the way to richness in life. It isn't about having all things our way but rather the simple trust in who He is and that who He said He was is who He truly is. He says He is enough. If we are so busy searching for answers, we will be led astray into a path that will not benefit us at all. He tells us to trust. Sometimes we get going so fast in our own way that we fail to see His warning signs as we fly past them at breakneck speed without taking time to heed. Take the time today to bank His promises into the deepest recesses of your heart where nothing can erode or devalue it. No matter what happens in your day, remember that He who was there with David is here with you. Ponder His morsels of wisdom. Be blessed in His ways of wise living. Transfer the wise counsel from His lips to yours. Carefully read the road-map of His word. Be single minded in pursuing Him over all else. Attentively watch what He is doing and relish it, even in the bad times. Remember His promises in the vault of your heart and do not let what is whirling around take control of your heart and mind.

If you don't know what you're doing, pray to the Father. He loves to help. You'll get his help, and won't be condescended to when you ask for it. Ask boldly, believingly, without a second thought. People who "worry their prayers" are like wind-whipped waves. Don't think you're going to get anything from the Master that way, adrift at sea, keeping all your options open.

James 1: 5-8

Adrift!

"If you don't know what you're doing, pray to the Father." It seems so simple and it is...yet we get so wrapped up, balked up by fear that our prayers are lacking in the boldness that activates faith. I remember my son when he was little, loved science and all the neat experiments we did in homeschooling. One of his favorites was the dry ice in the swimming pool. Water activates dry ice to bubble and smoke. He loved watching the chemical composition changes when hot water was thrown into the air on a cold day too. Prayers have power but their power is scoped by the faith that activates them. A little dry ice in the water only produces a little smoke. The more faith we throw into God's Living Water, the more our chemical makeup is changed and activated. Truly, this is an area that some people are gifted in, according to scripture. Some people are gifted with a larger measure of faith and others have the smallest amount but faith grows in action. A tiny mustard seed produces a huge crop when planted and watered. The amount of faith given does not determine the success of that faith, the amount active does. If I am given $100 then choose to invest nothing, I still have only $100. If I invest into a sure thing, I will reap rewards. The issue with us is the "sure thing". This is because we do not truly trust God to do as He says He will. We have the dry ice and we know the Living Water is there but we must put the ice into the water to make the change. It is scary. It leaves one completely open to God's will and not man's authority. It is a place of trust that we often do not get until we have no other choice. James says, "ask boldly, believingly, without a second thought"! This confidence is the all in, I believe no matter what kind of faith. I will always remember the instance of my son putting that first piece of dry ice into the pool. It was small in a vast amount of water so it smoked only a minute then went deep and was swallowed by the water. Did change still happen? Yes, absolutely, but we couldn't see it or experience it. As his dad lifted the whole chunk up with gloves and tongs, he watched and worried that it wasn't going to work. The ice was dropped into the pool and immediately sunk with no smoke. Boy was his disappointment palatable. He couldn't believe nothing happened. As he started to walk away in defeat, suddenly a cloud enveloped him. As he turned around, the waters were writhing and the smoke/bubbles were amazing...change was certainly evident then. As I think of this today, I ponder that many times we too drop our load of dry ice into the Living Waters then turn to walk away, disappointed that nothing happened as we expected it to be. We turn our backs on the One who promised change and miracles and provision because the timing wasn't ours. James says when we hedge our bets by worry and Plan B, C, D, instead of trusting, we are like wind whipped waves and this covers up the things that God is doing in our lives. Lord, I believe. I want to boldly walk in your ways and not be wind tossed with worry but to walk in holy confidence that you are who you said you are and your promises are true. You promised to be my provider and my source so I trust you to be exactly that. Help me Lord to ask boldly and believingly without a second thought. Boost my confidence God! Help me to invest the whole in You and not the little, due to lack of faith.

He told them, "You don't get to know the time. Timing is the Father's business. What you'll get is the Holy Spirit. And when the Holy Spirit comes on you, you will be able to be my witnesses in Jerusalem, all over Judea and Samaria, even to the ends of the world."

Acts 1: 7-8

Time!

Time is in His hands! This is the hardest and yet most simple concept of faith. We are not in control of the timing of our storms-not the duration of them nor the cessation of them as this is the Father's business. We are also not in control of end time events nor Jesus' return. We are in control of our actions and attitudes towards God's provision and timing and our mission. God has tasked each of us uniquely for His purpose of reaching others for Him and we are called for this solitary purpose. The power of the Holy Spirit is given to each of us to be witnesses through our storms. We have the ability to praise through our storms no matter what because He gave us the authority over our own human frailty. Our emotions may dictate anger, rage, hurt, disappointment and sorrow but our faith dictates a hope, a future and a promise. He never said there would only be good things and He never said there would be easy storms. He promised a heart of melody during the hard times as long as we are fixated on Him. We need to get our minds so set on Him that no matter what comes our way, we can still say He is God! Lord, I believe all things are possible! And then we can be about our mission despite the storms and through the trials. He only wants us centered on who He is, rather than what is happening, in order to move abundantly in our lives. It is hard to watch and wait in the hard times, because it feels like an endurance. But if we change our mindset from waiting for the other shoe to drop, to watching for what He is going to do in this storm, the waiting changes from endurance to anticipation. Anticipation is a whole different feeling and it is the same period of time but includes hope. God has given us a mission with a reward! Go into the world and tell all about who He is, especially during the storms. How we live through the storms matters to others and the calling. No, the timing isn't ours, but the mindset is. We need to move forth even in the impossible times in celebration of who He is. God gets all the glory for the outcome of our story so praise Him through it and watch Him do it!

"Don't let this rattle you. You trust God, don't you? Trust me. There is plenty of room for you in my Father's home. If that weren't so, would I have told you that I'm on my way to get a room ready for you? And if I'm on my way to get your room ready, I'll come back and get you so you can live where I live. And you already know the road I'm taking."

John 14: 1-4

Rattled!

The rattlesnake has a sound that it makes when it is about to strike as a warning to those around it. This sound is often unexpected and causes fear to inhibit the movement of the prey long enough to distract it from fleeing to safety. The definition of the word rattled is shaken to the core with fear and trepidation. There are plenty of things abounding now in our world to rattle us. My husband commented just a few days ago about how all things are blown up and immediately broadcast through social media, inspiring warnings, and often fear, more quickly than ever before. In particular we were discussing weather patterns and how news spreads so far and wide quickly yet often inaccurately or inadvisably. I am not against social media obviously as I post daily and use it as a ministry and business tool. I do think however that there is a lot of rattling that happens and causes harm in this medium as I see it too often in people. The enemy seeks to destroy the gift of peace and the walk of joyful contentment that we have in our Father. In John, Jesus is speaking to his disciples about the end times we live in today and He says, Don't! Don't let all this rattle you-Trust God! He instructs them to focus on His return and the eternal hope He promised rather than circumstances. This is HARDER than one thinks because the rattle of that old sneaky snake is loud, intimidating and very threatening in our lives from health to finances to emotional well being. The enemy is rattling at us to shake us into a place of fear and intimidation so that our focus moves from a place of peace in knowing who God is to a place of fear. Change and thoughts of the unknown intimidate the strongest person but God tells us to be of good cheer for no matter what happens or how bad it looks, no weapon formed against us will prosper and He has good things in store. We may have become a prisoner of our situations and choices. We may have been struck into fearful contemplation by the rattle of our circumstantial situations but rather than freezing in fear, it is time to praise the walls down and strike the fear of God into the enemy of our soul. Greater is He that is in me than He that is in this world! We are not subject to the destination of fear for we are promised an eternal hope. What He brings us to, He will bring us through. No matter how large our Red Sea is, He is still the wave talker and the wave walker! He will bring us through in victory if we will hold onto Him through it all!

Meanwhile, the eleven disciples were on their way to Galilee, headed for the mountain Jesus had set for their reunion. The moment they saw him they worshiped him. Some, though, held back, not sure about worship, about risking themselves totally.

Jesus, undeterred, went right ahead and gave his charge: "God authorized and commanded me to commission you: Go out and train everyone you meet, far and near, in this way of life, marking them by baptism in the threefold name: Father, Son, and Holy Spirit. Then instruct them in the practice of all I have commanded you. I'll be with you as you do this, day after day after day, right up to the end of the age."

Matthew 28: 16-20

Undeterred!

Ever been disappointed in God? Do you find yourself questioning His reasoning sometimes and not understanding His ways? This isn't sacrilegious, it's human. The disciples had just watched Jesus be crucified from a distance and were on the run from the religious crowd when they got the message that Jesus is alive and wants to meet with them. Naturally, they are on edge as if it is a trap, but then they saw Him. Immediately some were on their knees in worship but others held back, unsure of total commitment and risk. What I love about this story is that Jesus is undeterred by their skepticism and mistrust. He charged them in the great commission anyways. But more, He gave them and us the ultimate promise to be with us "day after day after day right up to the end of the age." Determination is setting the mind on a path and becoming unwavering in it. Being undeterred means not letting anything get in the way of that path. Jesus knew His charge and He knew those men and women as well as us intimately in that moment. He had already experienced the denial and betrayal of them so the doubt and insecurities they showed didn't startle Him nor make Him deliver less to them. This is an important lesson for us as we are often doubt filled skeptics that love God but have been "burned" by our faith in circumstances beyond our control where we feel let down. The disciples went from walking with Jesus in the victory of miracles to the roller coaster of running for their lives in denial of Him in mere days. Their whole world was shaken to the core. Everything they believed was questionable in their minds. They were feeling lost, bereft and let down. Then they get the message that Jesus is risen. They are too scared to hope but they go to meet Him anyways knowing what He said is possible and some had already seen Jesus. As they arrived at the mountain, some worshippers fell down in relief and awe while others still held onto their fear, hurt and insecurity. Jesus knows us! He knows we are scared to hope after things have been so bad. He knows we are insecure creatures lacking in open faith by nature. He created us with these fight/flight hormones. He knows us! Yet, He still gives us hope and promise and purpose despite our insecurities and inability to rest in who He is. He desires us to give complete trust and faith but His purpose and plans are undeterred by our mortal weaknesses. He is ready to use us despite ourselves and despite our focus on the situations or circumstances around us. Jesus gave His life for us despite our denials and betrayals. He willingly laid His life down and picked it up again to fulfill the law and then He gave His promise. We often feel like God has led us to a precipice and then left us but the reality is that He went before us. He wants us to step out in Faith knowing His promises and trusting in Him completely but He is undeterred by our lack. He desires our worship but He isn't weakened by our hesitation to trust. His purposes and plans are already in place. The difference is all about us. The worshippers who readily accepted who He is, was and will be, fell down in awe and acceptance, ready and at peace. The skeptics missed out. They still saw Jesus and received His promises and His charge but they missed the moments of worship, the peace of knowing, and the contentment of worshiping Him. Worshiping Him isn't just for Him. We know through research that worship actually releases endorphins in the brain that bring peace and tranquility to the mind and heart. Today we have a choice of trust and true worship. Will we worship Him the minute we see a glimpse of Him even if He seems to not be working or will we hold back, unsure about risking ourselves? It is our choice. The peace is there for our taking but we must step into worship to experience it. Jesus is undeterred. Nothing shakes Him, changes Him nor takes away His promises or purpose in our lives. No matter what we are experiencing, He is undeterred. Are we determined worshippers that will worship and watch for Him despite our battles? Will we be undeterred in our quest for Him?

A leper came to him, begging on his knees, "If you want to, you can cleanse me." Deeply moved, Jesus put out his hand, touched him, and said, "I want to. Be clean." Then and there the leprosy was gone, his skin smooth and healthy.

Mark 1: 40-41

Moved!

There are several times that scripture tells us that Jesus was deeply moved. He was moved with compassion when He saw the crowds wandering lost as sheep without a shepherd, moved with grief when He experienced the death of His friend, Lazarus and moved with anger when He saw the money changers in the Temple. We have seen Him moved by the faith of the woman with the issue of blood touching His garment and of the centurion with faith of Jesus' healing towards his assistant, but in this verse, Jesus was moved by one man's cry. "If you want to, you can." These are the words the man said to Jesus. As I attended an event recently, a discussion ensued about attendance and a comment was made that we do what we want to do. There is truth in this statement and we see it in this story. The leper appeals to Jesus to heal Him and Jesus says "I want to." There is such power in those words and in understanding that Jesus does want to. He desires more for us than we desire for ourselves. It is often so hard for us to look and see what He is saying to us. We hear the words but they don't align with our situation or circumstances so we get discouraged and think God just doesn't want to do what we need but the truth is far from that. You see the rest of the story is that Jesus knew His purpose and His mission was to change lives forever. He knew that as soon as He began healing, that throngs of crowds would come preventing Him from doing what He needed to accomplish in the mortal flesh. He told this leper to tell no one, but who can keep a secret like that? He immediately went out whole and told everyone, detailing all, and this derailed Jesus' journey as His compassion dictated that He heal all. Sometimes when things don't go our way, we think that God isn't able or He doesn't want to when in reality, often we are in our circumstances for another purpose. God isn't without means or ability. He doesn't lack compassion nor does He ignore our cries. He wants to do all that we ask or think which is why He charged us to be His hands extended. He has given us purpose, that very few of us are truly walking into as He directs. He desires that we become vessels of healing and miracles as we go through our days, operating in His power and authority. He desires for us to be His hands extended reaching out to the oppressed but we get caught up in our own daily troubles and sidelined so we cannot accompany our full purpose in Him. Then as He begins to work to remove these obstacles in our lives, we see Him as preventing us from having rather than He is growing us. It is important that we examine His want to. Scripture says Jesus was deeply moved. What moved Him? The sincerity of the faith of this leper moved Him. The leper recognized who Jesus was and knew what He could do. We are no less than this leper. Our aches and pains are no less important, neither are our other issues from finances to emotional well being. Whatever it is we are needing, only requires we ask because He wants to. He wants to heal you. He wants to baptize you. He wants to make you whole in every sense of that word. Perhaps the trials we are in are of our own making but this doesn't lessen His desire to make us whole. Lord, today, I know you want to touch my body, my finances, my business and my life. I know you want to. I know you can cleanse me and make me whole if you want to and I know you want to because you said it in your word. I ask today for miracles to abound. Backs healed, cancer gone, finances made whole, and emotional turmoil to cease. I know you want to and I claim this promise of want to, upon my life. Lord, I believe all things are possible and I am looking out towards the possibilities that you are bringing into fruition even now just because You want to be Lord of ALL in my life. I surrender all to Your authority and want to!

You realize, don't you, that you are the temple of God, and God himself is present in you? No one will get by with vandalizing God's temple, you can be sure of that. God's temple is sacred—and you, remember, are the temple.

1 Corinthians 3: 16-17

Present!

How often we go about our daily lives without glancing at the stars or taking time to see the dawn, not realizing that these are reminders of the present. The word present has many meanings but the meaning in this verse is evident and real. God is evident and real in us. Our bodies are home to the Most High. I watched the pomp and circumstance around the coronation recently and thought how over the top and majestic everything was. God Himself sits in splendor and majesty but chooses to reside in us also. We are a sacred temple of His dwelling yet often we fail to realize this. We see ourselves as just the human frailty of body without realizing that His Spirit has called us forth into a new awakening in Him. Night skies fascinate me because they are abundant with a show of light and twinkle but as I listened to an audiobook recently, I heard the author state that there are more stars than grains of sand. Wow! That is mind boggling. We who inhabit this planet are so finite in the scheme of life and our moments of celebration are so swiftly gone yet God Himself, the creator of all this majestic panorama takes the time to hear us, be with us, see us as we are and dwell in us. He is Present in us! Hurt and mistreatment, pain at the hand of others is not unseen nor unresolved. He said no one gets by with vandalism of God's temple and that is us. That makes us think a little longer and harder about how we treat others too because if we are His temple then so are they who love Him and are called by His purpose. Present. Current. Existing now. In this place. Here. Now. We are sacred; His. We are the dwelling place of the King of all creation. He is alive in us. The body is a miracle in all the little pieces and parts, from synapses firing to create thought, to the miracle of birth. We are unique, divine and His. Not because we are all that, but because He, that is all that, dwells in us. When I contemplate the stars and all the wonders of His hands, I am amazed that He chose me. That pain, rebuke it and cast it out of His temple. That hurt, tell it to be healed in Jesus' name. That loneliness, sit in it for a minute and begin to feel Him for He cares for you and dwells in you. That frustration, anger and bitterness, let it go. He cares more for you than any other and He is with you encouraging you to let it go.
Turn it over to Him and let Him make it right.

So, what do you think? With God on our side like this, how can we lose? If God didn't hesitate to put everything on the line for us, embracing our condition and exposing himself to the worst by sending his own Son, is there anything else he wouldn't gladly and freely do for us? And who would dare tangle with God by messing with one of God's chosen? Who would dare even to point a finger? The One who died for us—who was raised to life for us!—is in the presence of God at this very moment sticking up for us. Do you think anyone is going to be able to drive a wedge between us and Christ's love for us? There is no way! Not trouble, not hard times, not hatred, not hunger, not homelessness, not bullying threats, not backstabbing, not even the worst sins listed in Scripture: They kill us in cold blood because they hate you. We're sitting ducks; they pick us off one by one.
None of this fazes us because Jesus loves us. I'm absolutely convinced that nothing—nothing living or dead, angelic or demonic, today or tomorrow, high or low, thinkable or unthinkable—absolutely nothing can get between us and God's love because of the way that Jesus our Master has embraced us.

Romans 8: 31-39

Wedge!

I watched him cut the tree and still it stood unwavering. He cut again on the other side and yet she still stood strong. Then he applied a wedge and began to hammer it in giving more strength to one side than the other and began to tug with a pulley and winch which was roped around her. She swayed and seemed to try to remain steadfast but the load was too much, the wedge had changed her strength into a weakness as she leaned too far to accommodate it in the cut...she swayed, groaned then toppled with a resounding crash. The tug combined with the wedge... this is what gets us to topple and Satan knows this, but we have a promise. In Romans, Paul details the promise of God being on our side. He reminds us that God didn't hesitate to put His very best on our side, embracing the worst of humanity through the death and disparaging of His own son. Looking at that, is there any doubt that there is not anything that He would do for us? The One who died for us, is standing at this very moment making intercession for us to the Father because nothing stands in the way of His love for us. Wedges come in many forms and they separate us from the will of God in our lives causing us to weight shift and change our stance which is the beginning of the topple. Holding fast to the principles of God means that as the struggle comes, you are secure and fixed in Him. The old ways may cut on you and cause pain, sorrow and woes but they are not going to take you down. We need to learn to let go of the control and trust His leading even through the rough patches because His way is better even if we cannot see it. Read this passage of scripture, post it where you can affirm it in your life through every battle. Know that He is on our side and even if it looks like the devil is winning, He isn't, because greater is He that is in us than the gods of this world. No one can drive a wedge between us and God's love for us. Not even the worst of who we are is outside the love of God. Things may not look perfect in our lives. Times may get extremely difficult but the confidence in Him through it all is our promise. He is faithful and there is nothing to separate us from God's love. It comes down to the choice. The wedges of the world have been placed in our lifestyles. We can remove the wedges through prayer. We can refuse to accommodate that which would lead us away from Him.

Jesus said, "When you're celebrating a wedding, you don't skimp on the cake and wine. You feast. Later you may need to pull in your belt, but not now. As long as the bride and groom are with you, you have a good time. No one throws cold water on a friendly bonfire. This is Kingdom Come!"

Mark 2: 19-20

Skimp!

Walking in the surf while feeling the splash on my feet reminds me that there is an ocean but the edge is just the damp and occasional touch. To truly experience the ocean, you gotta be there and hear the roar, feel the waves and current around you. Experience is the best teacher but often not the most fun. People ask me how I know so much about breast cancer and I share that I have lived it through my mom's treatment but I haven't experienced it and never want to do so. Back pain I know, sepsis I know, surgeries I know, too many other health issues I know and I can say that I study about others but knowing and experiencing are different. Knowing about God and knowing God are different things. In Mark, Jesus has just healed a paraplegic man and He is being questioned by the religious leaders as to why He and His disciples do not fast as a religious observance. In His response, He states that while the bridegroom, meaning Himself, is present there is no need to fast but when He is taken away, then fasting is appropriate. These are the days of fasting. These are the days of trial and famine compared to those days of feast. We all walk through times of feast and famine in our lives. The times of famine or trial are the days of fasting. These are the times where one must know that God is because it is hard to see or feel His hand. These are the times where the waiting is the struggle. I think of the ocean with the continuous waves. The constant push of the water on the shore can be very calming to hear but that same constant push that calms one is a trial to another. Days go by that things seem bleak and the struggles are real for those with chronic pains. It is a hard struggle, but in the knowing is the difference. We know the waves are going out and coming back. There is a consistent anticipation of the next wave but the constant pressure is there. That knowing is a kind of peace. God is more than a wave in an ocean. He is a constant presence in our lives that is inviting change and sometimes that change isn't what we like. Sometimes the push is more than we can take and feels like a rip current taking us away from all we know, then we realize that fighting the current only wears us out. Instead, we need to be still, and begin to swim along the shore rather than towards the shore. We need to realize that the bridegroom is away preparing but He hasn't deserted the field. He left His authority with us in His Holy Spirit to be the witness through our trials and situations. Jesus Himself was beset with constant trial to the point of death while here on Earth. We all will have trials. He gave us examples and tools to understand these forces. He gave us His example. The process may not be fun or easy that we are walking in. The journey may not be a calming wave upon a shore that brings peace. It might be the strongest rip current we have ever experienced but He hasn't changed. He is still the wave walker. He says to Be still and know He is God even in the midst of the trials. Fast and pray as the Bridegroom is away but know that He hears us, sees us and is with us in Spirit and Truth. The waves may rip and pull today changing our landscape to an unrecognizable place but just on the other side, this ripping and pulling is a calming place of tranquil knowing. The knowing is the difference. Put away the panic and breathe. Know that no matter what happens, He is still God. Know that we are His and no good thing will He withhold from us if we walk in the knowledge of Him. The wave is just a wave. The rip currents are just a place of trial for a moment. He is still the one who says Peace, be still. The bridegroom is returning soon. Fix your eyes on this and only this. Find that place of knowing and swim in the direction of His horizon rather than against the rip current or trials. Let Him be God and we can be at peace in the knowing.

Jesus went on: "Does anyone bring a lamp home and put it under a bucket or beneath the bed? Don't you put it up on a table or on the mantel? We're not keeping secrets, we're telling them; we're not hiding things, we're bringing them out into the open.

"Are you listening to this? Really listening? "Listen carefully to what I am saying—and be wary of the shrewd advice that tells you how to get ahead in the world on your own. Giving, not getting, is the way. Generosity begets generosity. Stinginess impoverishes."

Mark 4: 21-25

Impoverished!

In Mark 4, Jesus is speaking plainly to his disciples about the difference in people who walk with Him and those in the world. He warns us to be careful of taking advice on how to get ahead in this world and instead to focus on giving. When things are hard, it is hard to dig deep to give. When we are going through tough times, we tend to turtle in and withhold our generosity as a way of self protection. The human instinct is to feather our own nest before sharing to others but this is counterintuitive to what God instructed. He said generosity breeds generosity and stinginess impoverishes. Listen, He says, really listen. All we have to do to see what God is doing is look at what Jesus did. He gave constantly and completely even to His own life. He was a giver and through this becomes a channel of God's gift in our lives. A lamp doesn't choose where to cast its light but throws it out to the whole. It doesn't choose who or what is worthy or unworthy of its glow and neither should we. We are not about being secretive or hiding the things of God but rather openly sharing His goodness and grace. We are to be His hands extended into the darkness. As I drove along the road, I saw a homeless man holding a sign. I had nothing to give except my lunch, so I rolled down my window and gave my all. Then instead of eating, I prayed for that man to come to know God. People say that he makes more begging at that intersection than you would think and that he isn't truly homeless. I say that is between him and God. It is easy to measure who blesses you and who doesn't with their presence and their presents. It is easy to see that, but hard to measure the ripple of the blessings we give. One drop of water dropped onto a mustard seed can be the difference in a crop of bounty. You don't have to have a lot to be generous in spirit. Truly, I can say that people have done me wrong many times. It is easy to count the negatives and see. It is also very humbling to see the truth in generosity because those gifts come back tenfold even when you cannot see it. Times may get challenging in our lives with economics and politics but we are not of this world. We need to be about the Father's business, finding ways to be used by Him in our marketplace of ministry. Lean into His ways, learn His rhythms and listen to Him speak. Are you listening? He asks.

So be content with who you are, and don't put on airs. God's strong hand is on you; he'll promote you at the right time. Live carefree before God; he is most careful with you.

1 Peter 5: 6-7

Live Carefree!

I have been dealing with this verse for over 4 months. I have pondered it in particular on the "carefree" part because I worry a lot and I let the cares of life weigh on me. I know I shouldn't. One of my favorite songs is Cast all your Cares on Him. But it is the statement, "Live Carefree before God", that I ponder. The statement has a dependent clause explaining why we should live carefree-because He is most careful with us. Meaning that God is filled with care for us so we can trust Him and know His hand is on us. So many times in these last few months, this verse has come up and I could not absorb it because I truly doubted it. "God's strong hand is on you", but again that dependence clause-He will promote you at the right time. As I prayed and this verse once again surfaced in my mind, I began to see the choice was there again. The promise is stayed as a command that the dependent clause is activated upon in our choice. We can choose the life with all our cares weighing upon us, keeping us beat down or we can choose to cast our cares upon Him. I think I have been fishing with my cares. I mean, I cast them but I left a line attached and kept slowly drawing them back into me with somehow more weight attached each time. I didn't cast my cares expecting to catch something that God had prepared that was great and purposeful. I cast my bait with an expectation of God failing me. That's a little hard to confess, but the truth is that I let disappointment in a situation that happened by my own choosing due to deception by another person, become a whale that swallowed me whole. Instead of praying inside that belly, I have been angry and whiny and frustrated and doubting and fickle. I have kneeled and cried and begged God to resolve it, but I haven't let it go. I have held onto that care like it is a lifeline instead of realizing that it was a trap. I hadn't made the choice to live carefree. The words to the old song rang through my mind over and over these last few months, "I care not today what tomorrow might bring whether shadow, or sunshine or rain. The Lord I know rules over all things and all of my worry is vain. Living by faith, in Jesus above. Trusting, abiding in His great love. From all harm safe in His sheltering arms, I'm living by faith and feel no alarm." This is carefree living. It is letting go of the safety harness. Letting go of the line of doubt and worry. It is complete trust in His "enough". I have no idea why we go through the things we do. I am sure there is some purpose but it is beyond my comprehension. What I do know is that I have a choice. I can choose to Live Carefree before God trusting in the dependent clause that He is most careful with me. I can lean into the promise that God's strong hand is on me and He will promote me at the right time. These promises are ours. It is our choice to embrace them and walk in them. I am choosing today to Live Carefree. I am going to write this verse upon my heart, the windows of my soul and around my home and workplaces. I am going to expect to be thrown up out of this whale's belly with a new purpose in God's provision.

I am looking forward to His Right Time because His hand is on Me!

Woke!

Matthew 1:20-25

We all have problems and dilemmas. We all have situations that dissatisfy, confuse, frustrate and leave us feeling lost and betrayed. We all have a choice when we wake up each day. What will we do about Jesus?

Key thought for today:

Right!
Matthew 2:9-10

Rightness =

Are you allowing God to use you, direct you and turn you into a shining light?

You may feel like your light is off and all is dark around you but His word dwells in you. Dig deep into His word and follow the instructions there. Listen to His voice as He speaks to you.

Key thought for today:

Fad!
Matthew 3:7-12

What counts is your life, is it green and flourishing?

How are you known? Do people see Jesus in you? Are you known by His love? Do you spend more time with Him than you do with the news/social media or YouTube/FB? Do people recognize you as His?

Fad or fade? Here's a hard question: would you go into this river full of alligators that is in the picture to be baptized with Him? This is the call of new anointing. Are we willing to sacrifice our own lives and lifestyles for more of Him? Fad, fade or Fire?

Key thought for today:

Test!
Matthew 4:4, 7, 10

Should we rely on our own physical strengths and emotions to drive us?

How does Jesus' example teach us to overcome and conquer any test?

Key thought for today:

Panoramic!

Matthew 5:17-20

God knows the most intimate details. We all have these moments of self awareness that shake our understanding of the world and realign us. Life is about moments....step back. Take a panoramic view of life rather than the moment you are in now. Give it all to Him....

Key thought for today:

Secluded!
Matthew 6:6-13

What does Matthew 6 tell us about approaching God?

Take time to be secluded in His peace and anchored in His presence, focus on who He is and allow Him to speak to your heart.

Key thought for today:

Initiative!

Matthew 7:12, 24-27

If I am building on God's word, how can I know that I am building on the rock and not the sand?

What is God's initiative?

Key thought for today:

Vanguard!
Matthew 8:10-12

Vanguard =

Faith =

So what is Vanguard Faith?

Key thought for today:

Whole!
Matthew 9:12-13, 20-22

Who needs Jesus?

If we can just touch Him in Faith believing, we will be made whole. What is whole?

Key thought for today:

Salinity!
Matthew 10:38-39

What is the reward that is promised, if we will turn it all over to Christ?

How do we get past the concept that the Church cannot stand up, for fear of being too salty?

Key thought for today:

Proof!

Matthew 11:16-19

Thomas was called Doubting...what are we called? What should we be called?

Why are we so easy to give up? Why do we who know who He is whine and cry so much? Why are we so opinion driven and short sighted in our faith vision?

Key thought for today:

Reckoning!
Matthew 12:6-8, 34-37

Our words have power and intent; If we use them carelessly, what will the consequence be?

How can we avoid such a tragedy?

Key thought for today:

Obedience!
Matthew 12:46-50

Obedience =

Who will you serve?

Will you choose to be a part of the family of God not because you are blood bought but because you choose to serve His will obediently?

Key thought for today:

Receptivity!
Matthew 13:11-17

How's your signal? Do you need to clear some debris or perhaps take blinders off or remove your fingers from your ears?
Prepare your own heart so that you might be blessed.

Key thought for today:

Curtains!

Matthew 13:37-43, 51-52

Why does Jesus ask the question, "Are you listening?"

Have you made a choice as to what your life behind the curtains will be?

Key thought for today:

Saved!

Matthew 14:28-31

How often do we say we will trust and believe?

No one is immune to the struggles of life, we're human, but what should our response be?

Key thought for today:

Pollution!
Matthew 15:10-11, 13-14, 16-20

How do the choices we make towards what others say and do affect us?

When we allow the heart to harbor things that are not of God, how does it affect our reactions? How do we become "HeartSmart"?

Key thought for today:

Access!

Matthew 16:19, 27-28

How do we gain free and complete access to God's kingdom?

What would you do if you had access to all of the money, all the power, and all of the means that you wanted? Would you use it to draw more people to Jesus or would it lead you in a path where you were focused on something other than Him?

Are you using all of your resources to lead others to Jesus now?

Key thought for today:

Move!

Matthew 17:5, 17-18, 20

Many seeds I plant but few I expect to germinate and be fruitful rather than expecting all. Why?

What is it about weeds that they always germinate?

What would happen if we woke up saying Lord, I believe and acted on it? What would happen if we fertilized the mustard seed of faith daily by speaking the words of life and beauty, watering it with His living water of the word?

Key thought for today:

Established!

II Thessalonians 3:3-5

What establishes us when the going gets tough?

What directs our hearts into patience?

Key thought for today:

Elemental!
Matthew 18:2-7

Simple and Elemental =

Different and Unique =

What is Jesus saying about the teaching of His word?

Key thought for today:

Centered!
Matthew 18:18-20

Have you considered the weight your words and the power they have?

Our words come from the abundance of our heart; Are your words casting life or death to your dreams, your family, your mission-fields of ministry?

Key thought for today:

Largeness!
Matthew 19:11-12

Why did Jesus call it..."growing into the largeness of marriage"?

What exactly does this largeness do for us?

Key thought for today:

Crestfallen!
Matthew 19:21-22

What is it that you cannot bear to let go of?

What is the evidence of us breaking free of the bounds of Earth?

Key thought for today:

Lavish!

2 Corinthians 9:6-7

Why did Jesus use a mustard seed as an example of faith?

The sowing is:

The waiting is:

The trusting is:

Remember. Lavish sowing gets a lavish harvest but what we sow matters. What are you planting in the lives of others around you?

Key thought for today:

Worthy!
Psalms 3:3

Are you tired of fighting it all? Have you cried out to Him? Are you trusting the process?

When we cry out to Him in desperation, how does He respond?

Key thought for today:

Fair!
Matthew 20:13-16

Why should we strive to make the best of whatever circumstance arises in our life?

Is it fair that God's only son sacrificed His life as an atonement for our sins?

Is any of us truly more worthy than another of that sacrifice?

The true measure of equality or fairness is….

Key thought for today:

Used!
Matthew 7:26-27

Have you ever been used up and tossed aside by another person as if you didn't matter? Using and not acting upon God's word is an example of this lack of understanding. How does this compare to the person who doesn't choose a firm foundation to build upon?

How do we establish a solid foundation so that no matter what comes our way we can weather the storms?

Key thought for today:

Sight!
Matthew 20:29-34

What did the blind men do when the crowd tried to hush them?

If we want to deeply move the heart of God to hear our cry, what must we do?

Key thought for today:

Triumph!
Matthew 21:21-22

The large things we implore, intercede and believe for but Jesus works in the small things too. Nothing big or small is impossible for God. What is it that we are needing in our lives?

Key thought for today:

Picked!
Psalms 4:1, 3-8

What are you seeking more of in your daily routine? More peace and joy or more of something to complain about? Have you made your case before Him?

Key thought for today:

Robust!
Philippians 3:7-9

God tells us that His power is alive in us and Paul describes it as robust. Does it mean we don't have trouble in this world?

Paul who had experienced his share of it for sure said that he counts all the good as loss and is more than happy to suffer for Christ. Why?

What did Jesus say was the most important thing in life?

Key thought for today:

Profit!
Mark 8:35-37

Jesus was willing to give His life for your soul and He did. But what are you willing to give up?

We get caught up in our situations and desires and futures and wants, striving to gain it all. At what cost? Is that one thing you desire worth your soul?

What does it profit a person to gain all but lose their soul? What is the thing, dream, hope, etc. that you are putting ahead of God in your life? What are you willing to lay down for Him?

Key thought for today:

Titles!
Matthew 23:8-12

Are you struggling with all the "hats" or roles that you have? What did Jesus say in Matthew about allowing people to put us on a pedestal?

Key thought for today:

Promises!
Matthew 23:16-22

Define Promise:

Scripture tells us that men and women are fickle promise keepers but God always keeps His word. People often get confused by the why and the wait. Why does God let bad things happen to good people and when is God going to come through on His promises? How can we encourage one another in the waiting?

Key thought for today:

Worn!
Matthew 24:13-14, 32-35

Are you tired? Worn? Heavy? Take it to Jesus.
Despite everything that happens in this world, What does God's word say when you feel like giving up?

Key thought for today:

Anticipation!
Matthew 24:39-44

Are you ready? Are your eyes on Him and His soon return? Be vigilant because it can happen at any moment!

Define in your own words how you are preparing in Anticipation of His return.

Key thought for today:

Vigilant!
Proverbs 4:23-27

Define Vigilant:

What is our most valuable treasure?

What is a vigilant watch over our hearts?

Key thought for today:

Enter!
Matthew 25:34-36

Why do we tend to forget about His blessings in the midst of our struggles?

God Himself, the King of all Glory has called us His blessed because we are His and He charges us with a task to use these blessings to minister to others. What are these ministries?

Key thought for today:

Vigil!
Matthew 26:36-39

Define Vigil:

What is the root of betrayal?

What do you need to surrender? What have you placed on the altar of self which has taken precedence over Him?

What is your vigil? What is the thing worth staying awake in time of sleeping?

Is He worthy of your vigil? Your sacrifice?

Key thought for today:

Able!

Matthew 26:52-54

Why is it so important for us to grasp the understanding of choosing to fight/flight?

What gives us the ability to yield our will and allow God to fight our battles?

Key thought for today:

Reality!
John 1:9-13

Who does the Word say the "Begotten of God" are?

Do you believe, no matter what?

Key thought for today:

Knotted!

Psalms 143:7-10

We get spun up and stuck in our own messes and then we are so stirred up that we keep making our situations worse until they hit the place of the impossible.

How do we get ourselves out of the impossible situations we get ourselves into?

Key thought for today:

Precious!
Proverbs 31:10-12, 25-26, 30-31

What is it that you are holding onto? Give it all to Him and He will make it worth far more than rubies.

Key thought for today:

Abandoned!
Matthew 27:45-46, 51-53

Are you feeling bereft and abandoned?
Faith walking requires uncertainty in circumstances but certainty in Him who is able.
Can you list any other examples of Faith Walkers in the bible? In your life?

Are You ready to start your "Faith Walk"?

Key thought for today:

Bankrupt!
Psalms 119:9-16

Why did God say David was a man after His own heart?

Are you pursuing the promises of God and banking His word into your heart?

Key thought for today:

Adrift!

James 1:5-8

Are you walking boldly in his ways or are you lacking the faith needed to stand and trust God to do as He says He will? Activate your faith today and stand on His promises!

Key thought for today:

Time!

Acts 1:7-8

Are you waiting for the other shoe to drop, or watching for what He is going to do in anticipation?

Anticipation is....

Key thought for today:

Rattled!
John 14:1-4

Rattled:

Are you allowing the enemy to get you rattled?

What does God tell us to do when fear tries to raise its head?

Key thought for today:

Undeterred!

Matthew 28:16-20

Have you ever been disappointed in God? Do you find yourself questioning His reasoning sometimes and not understanding His ways?

Will you worship Him the minute you see a glimpse of Him even if He seems to not be working or will you hold back, unsure about risking yourself? It is your choice.

Key thought for today:

Moved!
Mark 1:40-41

Scripture says Jesus was deeply moved. What moved Him?

We are no less than this leper. Our aches and pains are no less important, neither are our other issues from finances to emotional well being. Whatever it is we are needing, only requires we ask because He wants to.

Key thought for today:

Present!

I Corinthians 3:16-17

We are the dwelling place of the King of all creation. He is alive in us. He said no one gets by with vandalism of God's temple and that is us. Take those hurts, frustrations, anger and bitterness to Him and let Him make it right.

Key thought for today:

Wedge!
Romans 8:31-39

In Romans, Paul details the promise of God being on our side. He reminds us that God didn't hesitate to put His very best on our side, embracing the worst of humanity through the death and disparaging of His own son. Looking at that, is there any doubt that there is not anything that He would do for us?

Key thought for today:

Skimp!

Mark 2:19-20

We need to realize that the bridegroom is away preparing but He hasn't deserted the field. Fast and pray as the Bridegroom is away but know that He hears us, sees us and is with us in Spirit and Truth.

Key thought for today:

Impoverished!

Mark 4:21-25

We need to be about the Father's business, finding ways to be used by Him in our market-place of ministry. Lean into His ways, learn His rhythms and listen to Him speak. Are you listening? He asks.

Key thought for today:

Live Carefree!
I Peter 5:6-7

Are you ready to let it all go and live carefree in trusting that He is enough and that in His right timing He will bring you out?

What are you willing to let go of today?

Key thought for today:

* 9 7 9 8 9 9 9 1 6 1 6 4 1 6 *